THE
VAN GOGH
BLUES

THE
VAN GOGH
BLUES

THE CREATIVE PERSON'S PATH
THROUGH DEPRESSION

ERIC MAISEL, PH.D.

RODALE

Printed in the United States of America

Rodale Inc. makes every effort to use acid-free (∞), recycled paper (♻).

Cover and Interior Designer: Christopher Rhoads
Cover Photographer: Francis G. Mayer/CORBIS

Library of Congress Cataloging-in-Publication Data

Maisel, Eric, date.
  The Van Gogh blues : the creative person's path through depression / Eric Maisel.
        p.   cm.
  Includes bibliographical references and index.
  ISBN 1–57954–570–X hardcover
  1. Depression, Mental.   2. Personality and creative ability.   3. Artists—Mental health.   4. Artists—Psychology.   I. Title.
  RC537 .M335   2002
  616.85'27—dc21   2002006686

Distributed to the book trade by St. Martin's Press

2   4   6   8   10   9   7   5   3   1   hardcover

Visit us on the Web at www.rodalestore.com, or call us toll-free at (800) 848-4735.

WE **INSPIRE** AND **ENABLE** PEOPLE TO IMPROVE
THEIR LIVES AND THE WORLD AROUND THEM

For Ann, my true partner

CONTENTS

PREFACE

I began writing my first novel in 1971, when I was 24, after I graduated from the University of Oregon with an undergraduate degree in philosophy. For the next decade, I lived the novelist's life, smoking two-and-a-half packs of cigarettes a day, and frequented coffeehouses and pubs in Dublin, London, Paris, Budapest, Greenwich Village, San Francisco, and other existential locales. I ghostwrote books on every oddball subject from scientific nonfiction to medical thrillers and mysteries, earned a master's degree in creative writing from San Francisco State University, and wrote many novels, some of which were published by small presses.

Then I settled down. I trained to become a psychotherapist, earning three additional degrees: an undergraduate degree in psychology, a master's in counseling, and a Ph.D. in counseling psychology. I became a nationally certified counselor and a licensed marriage and family therapist and, since I loved them, worked exclusively with creative and performing artists. I also began to write nonfiction in the area of creativity and have had a dozen books on that subject published since 1990.

Imperceptibly, the work I was doing began to shift away from traditional psychotherapy and toward a branch of helping I began to call creativity coaching. I found myself uninterested in diagnosing supposed mental illnesses according to prescribed formulae. What engrossed me was working with a creator's totality, everything from her anxieties to her marketing skills, her blues to her creative processes. Still in its infancy, creativity coaching is a field I have helped to invent and shape and one that right now is more dream than reality. Few trained creativity coaches yet exist. In recent years, I have begun training new creativity coaches, and we shall see if this helping profession sets roots and becomes a full-fledged career option.

In the early 1980s, I became interested in Vincent van Gogh: van Gogh the painter, van Gogh the individual, van Gogh the icon of the tortured artist, and van Gogh the representative of universal themes in the lives of creators. I gave my first presentation on van Gogh at the 1987 Creativity and Madness Conference in Aspen, Colorado, in a talk entitled "Loving Blue: Meaning in Van Gogh's Firmament." I accompanied my talk with slides of van Gogh's landscape paintings to remind the audience that painted blue skies—mere pigment on canvas—could cry out with meaning. From those days until today, I have been chewing on the ideas presented in this book.

Here, I am drawing on many sources: my work as a psychotherapist and creativity coach; information presented to me by readers of my monthly creativity newsletter (read by some thousands); reports from the creativity coaches I train; conversations with friends and acquaintances in the arts, sciences, and business; feedback from conference and workshop participants; my reading of the psychology, creativity, and existential literature; and, of course, from my life in the arts. It may not always be clear whether I am talking about a client in therapy, a creativity coaching client, an artist of my acquaintance, a newsletter reader, or a creativity coach I've trained, but I hope that any confusion is minimal.

This is not a book about van Gogh. He appears, disappears,

reappears, but he never settles down as our central subject or object. Rather, this is a book about all creators: about you, me, painters in Tokyo, biologists in Moscow, novelists in Egypt. It is about who we are, what we do, and why we get depressed. Obliquely, it is about the meaning in literal blue skies and in the blue skies of paintings. Directly, it is about the heroism required of creators. I hope this book will help you and support you when meaning starts to fail and depression stealthily creeps in.

THE
VAN GOGH
BLUES

INTRODUCTION

I imagine that you are a creative person or a would-be creative person who has experienced bouts of depression in the past, who may be depressed right now, or who knows that you have the seeds of depression growing in you. You may have tried psychotherapy or antidepressant drugs, but you probably remain unconvinced that the answers you are looking for about the causes and management of your depression can be supplied by psychologists or medical doctors alone. If you are in this situation, this book is for you.

In this book, I provide what I believe is a new, more accurate picture of why creative individuals are prone to depression and describe a plan for managing creator's depression. This plan is comprised of several core tasks that you can immediately implement in your life. Even if you avail yourself of therapy, antidepressant drugs, support groups, spiritual practices, or other treatments for your depression, you will still need to master the tasks I outline in this book if you are going to deal effectively with your creator's depression.

The cliché is that creativity and depression go hand-in-hand. Like many clichés, this one is quite true. But creators are not necessarily afflicted with some biological disease or psychological disorder that causes them to experience depression at the alarming rates that we see. They experience depression simply because they are caught up in a struggle to make life seem meaningful to them. People for whom meaning is no problem are less likely to experience depression. But for creators, losses of meaning and doubts about life's meaningfulness are persistent problems—even the root causes of their depression.

The psychiatrist Arnold Ludwig studied a thousand eminent 20th century figures. In *The Price of Greatness*, he concluded that in his sample, 77 percent of the poets, 54 percent of the fiction writers, 50 percent of the visual artists, and 46 percent of the composers had suffered from at least one significant depressive episode. By contrast, the rate was 16 percent for sports figures, 5 percent for military figures, and zero percent for explorers. But Ludwig's numbers for creators are low because virtually 100 percent of creative people will suffer from episodes of depression.

Why virtually 100 percent? Because every creative person came out of the womb ready to interrogate life and determine for herself what life would mean, could mean, and should mean. Her gift or curse was that she was born ready to stubbornly doubt received wisdom and disbelieve that anyone but she was entitled to provide answers to her own meaning questions. Was she the only baby born on that day that way, with that gift or curse? No one can say. Nature-versus-nurture questions are unanswerable, except in superficial ways. What is clear is that some people grow up doubting and questioning while the majority don't. These meaning investigators are our creators, and they are prone to meaning crises and consequent depression by virtue of the fact that they find meaning a problem and not a given.

The depression they experience may be entirely existential or it may be an add-on existential depression, added on to some already-existing biological or psychological depression. Again, we don't know and can't know at this time what exactly is going on. We don't even know what we mean by "biological depression" or "psychological depression." Since there is so much that we do not know, you must take the following advice to heart: Even if your depression is primarily rooted in meaning problems, that should not stop you from seeking medical treatment.

Antidepressant drugs work for many people, creators included, to reduce their experience of depression. It is therefore important that you think about including them in your personal treatment plan. Antidepressant drugs can be lifesavers and can serve you even if your depression is mild, even if what you are experiencing is more anxiety than depression, and even if their rationale for use is obscure or faulty.

But drugs are not the only answer, and they are certainly not the complete answer. I have seen even serious depression lift after only one creativity coaching session. Over the course of 20 years of counseling and coaching creative clients, I have witnessed this recovery happen time and again. It happens because a client recognizes that she has meaning problems to tackle. Simply by glimpsing the territory she must traverse, she regains hope, a renewed sense of purpose, and a clearer picture of what steps she must take in her creative life. Nor do these gains last for only a day or a week. I have heard from clients a year or two after a single session that something important happened that had not faded away.

Creators have trouble maintaining meaning. Creating is one of the ways they endeavor to maintain meaning. In the act of creation, they lay a veneer of meaning over meaninglessness and sometimes produce work that helps others maintain meaning. This is why creating is such a crucial activity in the life of a creator: It is one of the ways, and often the most important way, that she manages to make life feel meaningful. Not creating is depressing because she is not making meaning when she is not creating. Creating but falling short in her efforts is also depressing because only insufficient meaning is produced if her products strike her as weak or shallow. Even creating well can be depressing because of the lingering sense that what she is doing is only veneering meaninglessness.

These are some of the intricacies we must examine. Our subjects are how meaning comes and goes, how meaning can be made and maintained, and how creating and meaning-making are related. It is only by recognizing the preeminent place of "meaning-as-problem" in the lives of creators that the depression they experience is explicable.

Listen, for example, to the following reports from four creators. Try to imagine what a biochemist or a psychiatrist would make of them. In fact, no biological or psychological approach can make heads or tails of these reports. Only an existential approach will do.

Roccie Hill, novelist, nonprofit administrator, and friend, wrote:

> Oh, Eric, does anyone really believe that depression and creativity do not go hand-in-hand? Depression is a sign of the onslaught of creativity—the wheels are spinning and digging deeper and deeper and as they dig, before creativity pulls it all together—that is depression. After the creative moment, that's euphoria. But before, it's always depression. It's a sign, as is the euphoria. That's all. You can't take any of it seriously—riding out the depression without trying to escape it (trying to escape it means you lose the creative moment) is what is important. Being euphoric without annoying your friends too much, until it passes . . . because the important thing is the creative moment.

Donna Riddlebarger, social worker, writer, and designer, explained:

> First of all, I think depression is a form of wealth. I believe having access to our own emotions is a gift that some folks lose at an early age, and others medicate away with a variety of distractions. I've observed many people who appear to fake their way

through adult life with forced smiles and feigned happiness. My radar says that they're faking it so that they can keep looking strong and powerful, in control, invulnerable to grief and sadness. I always wonder if they take off their smile when they go behind private doors since the cheer often appears to be put on like a nice suit.

I read somewhere that we begin grieving the instant we're born because we've given up the only tangible security we can ever have. That is to say that loss, fear, and anger—major components of grief—are intended to be ever-present in a human life. Depression evolves when we stop expressing our genuine emotions. Perhaps that occurs as we learn to put on a happy face to please those who feed us, tickle our chin, and touch us when we look cute and happy. I freely admit that I would walk toward a happy baby, or adult, faster than toward one who's screaming. And so the socialization begins. Be easy, be happy, or be rejected. Don't let others know how you see things, or how you feel, if it jeopardizes your crumbs of security. Some would rather give up expression than risk being or feeling alone.

I also believe that those who are the most creative are those willing to see their own soul, to be touched by their own spirit. Artists are people who fundamentally want answers to the hardest questions; i.e., to know more about who they are and why they are here. To be creative often means being brave enough to contemplate our own creation and get those answers. And for that, you'll eventually have to risk a little solitude, a little fear and confusion, and perhaps a little depression as a result of engaging the unknown.

Joan Woodward, a stained glass artist, wrote:

I cannot imagine being a creative soul without cycles of good healthy depression. For myself it has been with me from my earliest years. My mother told me that at age 4 I had a little suitcase and would put all of my drawings in it, put it away, then later get it out and spend a lot of time looking at each drawing. When I was 12, my mother would know I was depressed when I went to my room, closed the door, and played the violin without being told to practice.

Some days when I'm depressed I hear myself saying, "This can't be happening to me; I have been through this so many times before." Observing the pattern within the process, I attempt to become mindful, switch gears, and breathe into a different approach to the moment. In the early years it was difficult to bear myself after large creative expressions. One time, after six or eight months of putting myself aside to allow windows for an Episcopal church to come into being, after they were installed and blessed, it was an experience of death and then rebirth. Even now I shudder at what emotions I went through. But I have come to understand the nature of the experience.

Caroline Bertorelli, an artist, observed:

I get depressed quite regularly and often. It used to distress and frustrate me that I have such a tendency. But as I grow older, I see my depression as a valuable time for introspection and deep thinking about life. When I am not depressed, I can be fairly active in terms of work and getting things done, as well as being physically active cleaning the house or whatever. But being depressed gives me time out to be an observer of things that are happening around me and to me. I now just accept it as part of my personality. Sometimes I'm up and sometimes I'm down. When I'm up, that's my time for getting things done, solving problems, and being productive. When I'm down, that's my time for taking things more slowly and thinking— and in a way I'm grateful for that.

The common thread running through these four reports is an awareness on the creator's part that her depression is not an illness. Rather, it is the inevitable result of her experience of the facts of existence and her need to find and fashion meaning. It is not wealth or blessing, either, but it is easy to see why a creator might reframe it as such. What she knows for certain is that it isn't a disease. Rather, it is a state of affairs tied up with her efforts to create and to matter.

LISTENING FOR MEANING CRISES

If you listen to how creative people characterize their depression, you will hear clues about the causes of their difficulties. Sometimes the clues are subtle, and sometimes they stare you in the face. An example of the latter is the following, from Leo Tolstoy:

> Five years ago a strange state of mind began to grow upon me: I had moments of perplexity, of a stoppage, as it were, of life, as if I did not know how I was to live or what I was to do. These stoppages of life always presented themselves to me with the same questions: "why?" and "what for?" These questions demanded an answer with greater and greater persistence and, like dots, grouped themselves into one black spot. Well, what if I should be more famous than Gogol, Pushkin, Shakespeare, Molière—than all the writers in the world—well, and what then? I could find no reply. Such questions demand an immediate answer; without one it is impossible to live. Yet answer there was none. I felt that the ground on which I stood was crumbling, that there was nothing for me to stand on, that what I had been living for was nothing, that I had no reason for living. The truth was, life was meaningless.

The following is a much subtler self-report. It is the suicide note left by the painter Ralph Barton:

> Everyone who has known me and who hears of this will have a different hypothesis to offer to explain why I did it. Practically all of these hypotheses will be dramatic—and completely wrong. Any sane doctor knows that the reasons for suicide are invariably psycho-pathological. Difficulties in life merely precipitate the

event—and the true suicide type manufactures his own difficulties. I have had few real difficulties. I have had, on the contrary, an exceptionally glamorous life—as lives go. And I have had more than my share of affection and appreciation. The most charming, intelligent, and important people I have known have liked me—and the list of my enemies is very flattering to me. I have always had excellent health. But, since my early childhood, I have suffered with a melancholia which, in the past five years, has begun to show signs of manic-depressive insanity. It has prevented my getting anything like the full value out of my talents, and, for the past three years, has made work a torture to do at all. It has made it impossible for me to enjoy the simple pleasures of life that seem to get other people through. I have run from wife to wife, from house to house, and from country to country, in a ridiculous effort to escape from myself. In doing so, I am very much afraid that I have spread a good deal of unhappiness among the people who have loved me.

Everything that a person might want to think about with respect to creativity and depression is embedded in this suicide note. Barton expresses the contemporary stress-diathesis hypothesis nicely: that difficulties (stressors) precipitate depression in a person "disposed" to being depressed. He then adds the cognitive fillip: that we manufacture our own difficulties. He puts the interpersonal model of depression on the table and rejects it, arguing that it wasn't from a lack of human contact that his depression arose. (Though we are free to speculate whether he found those relationships as meaningful as he claims them to have been.) His "running from wife to wife, house to house, and country to country" will make the biologically inclined observer murmur, "Ah, there's the mania! Bipolar disorder!" Anyone looking for a psychodynamic explanation will be cheered by his admission that his affliction must be "psycho-pathological."

There is meat for a whole textbook in Barton's suicide note. But what should strike us as most important is the innocent phrase "as

lives go" in the sentence "I have had, on the contrary, an exceptionally glamorous life—as lives go." This phrase is the key to the matter.
It is an ironic indictment of life itself, an understated announcement
that the facts of existence could not be made to mean. Barton says
that there are no reasons outside of himself that explain his depression; he asks that we do not search for any external circumstances
that caused his malaise—no one and nothing did it to him. He sup-
poses that the reasons for his depression must be psychological and
constitutional. But he knows better.

If we questioned Barton, eventually he might admit that he had
been laid low by his inability to find and sustain meaning. To that
honest reply we might wonder whether, when he said that many
people had liked him and loved him, he meant by that careful phrase
that he hadn't actually liked or loved any of them in return. We might
probe the connection between meaninglessness and lovelessness and
wonder whether he might have found life worth living if he'd loved
more fully, people and painting both, and perhaps in that order. In
short, we would put a new idea on the table: that if Barton could have
found meaning in life—later we will say, if he could have "forced life
to mean"—he would have healed his depression and saved his life.

THE TASK OF MEANING-MAKING

What sort of task is the task of meaning-making? The painter Dianne
Albin summed it up beautifully:

> As a woman and an artist, and also having reached my 50th
> year, I find I have many questions about the life I have chosen.
> Having searched the literature on what it means to be an artist, on
> what it means to be creative, I am no less puzzled. As with art, there
> is no all-embracing answer or point of view. And perhaps that is the

crux of this paradoxical life. We embrace a life of solitude in order to embrace our creativity. We live outside the mainstream of life and struggle endlessly to survive both emotionally and financially. And we wonder why do we do this thing that causes so much pain and also joy.

In seeking therapy for a bout of depression, I began to search for answers and then better questions. Both the depression and the deep creative block I was experiencing prodded me ruthlessly to find some meaning in my dilemma, some way to survive the ordeal and heal the wounds if possible. Most self-help books were too shallow and offered merely a Band-Aid remedy to deeper issues, while current psychology was a theoretical nightmare. From the many bits and pieces, I did garner a pair of essential questions. Why have I chosen this life and to what end? Obviously, it wasn't for financial gain or success, as measured by contemporary values. Nor can I say the endless solitude or financial dependence is something one would actually choose if given a more practical, thoughtful moment. What then is the answer? Whom can I ask?

In the end, I think it is the search for the real, but also the search for the self, the search for what it means to be human. Perhaps this will sound trite to many, but it really is that simple, I'm afraid. With the dawning of human consciousness, the search for meaning entered the equation of survival. It was not enough to have food and shelter; the questions of who am I and what is it that brings meaningfulness to life also became significant. It is our ability to think and feel, I believe, to see beyond the immediate concerns of the given moment that plunges us into an eternal search that seems to defy our finite existence. We are limited by our frailties, our fears, and yet we pursue the endless question to find some meaning.

For an artist, it is a driven pursuit, whether we acknowledge this or not, that endless search for meaning. Each work we attempt poses the same questions. Perhaps this time I will see more clearly, understand something more. That is why I think that the attempt always feels so important, for the answers we encounter are only partial and not always clear. Yet at its very best, one work of art, whether produced by oneself or another, offers a sense of possibility that flames the mind and the spirit, and in that moment we know this is a life worth pursuing, a struggle that offers the possibility of answers as well as meaning. Perhaps in the end, that which we seek lies within the quest itself, for there is no final knowing, only a continual unfolding and bringing together of what has been discovered.

For years I have struggled with discovering my own voice as an artist, a way of seeing that came from deep within myself, that belonged to no other. Why this deep and abiding need to have one's own voice, one's own vision? This struggle in itself has proven more difficult than I could ever have imagined. Why this need to separate and distinguish my deepest self, my own true thoughts, feelings, and beliefs from the accepted norm of society? That, I think, has been both the gift and burden of human consciousness. As much as we cling to one another and desire to be part of our human group, we know that we are truly separate. For all the many devices we utilize, we can never quite overcome our separateness.

We find some solace in our groups of shared belief, thinking this will mollify the sense of isolation, and to some extent it does. But as we grow older the question "Is that all there is?" becomes more paramount, more insistent. For those called to the life of an artist, this question of meaning, of singular identity, comes sooner rather than later. My own experience came at the somewhat early age of six when I encountered the artwork of another. What was it that I experienced at an age when I lacked the words or understanding to process this encounter?

In time I have come to understand more clearly that what I felt was quite simply that I was not alone—separate perhaps, but not alone. That there were those who had the capacity and ability to invest paint, canvas, stone with our deepest feelings, thoughts, and *experiences and make an art that both embraced and explored our humanity. To create, to express the depth and experience of our consciousness of being alive, all the while knowing that death hovers nearby, that is what we do. If all this sounds a bit esoteric, I can only suggest that after we fill our bellies and find shelter from the raging elements, we occasionally pause—and in that pause we desire more than anything to understand and feel our humanness and perhaps see more clearly, if only for a moment, the wonder that surrounds us.*

I can only shudder when I think of life without our handiwork. The sheer paucity of living only for the sake of survival and empty diversion would be that of an empty vessel. My own life as an artist helps me to fill that vessel, and on occasion I am able to share that with another. Is there meaning in my struggle, my endless solitude? Yes, I believe there is, for at the very least I have found greater meaning for myself in that search. And as those artists who have come before me have perhaps more clearly expressed, our ability to ponder the questions that denote our humanness are worthy of a life of solitude. That is where I find my solace and my courage. In the final analysis, it is the art that I make that allows me to pause and briefly see. Only now do I begin to understand and accept both the burden and joy of my life.

PREVAILING THEORY

How does prevailing theory define depression? Essentially, it calls it an illness with biological, psychological, and/or social roots. More a hodgepodge of contradictory ideas than a coherent theory, it raises essential questions without making a diligent enough effort to answer them. How, for instance, can a given person's depression be called biological by one clinician and psychological by another? More telling, how can these two conflicting diagnoses not cause the pair of clinicians to chat, compare notes, and think through whether the depression they are witnessing is more an apple or more a pear?

Robert Klitzman, in his book *In a House of Dreams and Glass*, describes one corner of this odd world, the corner that psychiatrists inhabit. Here, two entirely different and discrepant explanations, one biological and one psychological, can routinely be provided to explain the exact same phenomenon. For instance, a woman visits the young intern Klitzman for treatment of her depression. After the initial consultation, Klitzman meets with each of his two supervisors, describes his new patient, and asks for their advice. Provided with a few-sentence description of the woman, the first supervisor, biologically inclined, asserts that the patient's problem is biological. The second supervisor, psychologically inclined, asserts that the patient's problem is psychological. Klitzman shakes his head and goes off to pursue both courses of treatment, hoping that he is not Alice and that this is not Wonderland. Klitzman explained:

> This case taught me a lot. My supervisors' initial expectations and plans had to be dropped. What worked with my patient in the end was neither a psychological nor a psychopharmacological approach. In short, the effectiveness of treatments couldn't be accurately predicted. They would have to be tried. That may sound obvious, but each supervisor had presented his approach to me as if it were clearly right, supported by theories and explanations, and guaranteed to succeed. However, solutions might be evident only after each approach had been attempted. Even then, neither might work. Moreover, the two different approaches—psychodynamic and biological—each sought to achieve the same outcome. I didn't understand how.

Both the biological and psychological approaches are suspect since both posit an unreal world, completely at odds with human experience, in which people do not get depressed for good reasons having to do with their experience of life and their uneasiness about the facts of existence. Rather, people only get depressed because something in them is flawed or broken. Depression of any magnitude, these approaches claim, is always an illness and never a reaction to being dropped, willy-nilly, into a world not of their making, which they are forced to make mean something.

The biological approach can prove very effective and alluring. Using drugs to manipulate neurotransmitting chemicals and hormones often works, just as electrically activating a rat's pleasure center will make him think that he is having a great day. But practitioners of the biological approach do not know as much as they would like us to believe that they know. Their methods often work because they directly manipulate the concomitants of mood. You may still be depressed but no longer feel depressed, and that can be both a benefit and a blessing.

One must be equally wary of the psychological approach. One psychotherapist may espouse one thing while another espouses the exact opposite. A neo-Freudian says that personality is meant to develop and if it doesn't, we become ill. A neo-Jungian argues that we are born whole and that troubles arise because we undevelop, especially during the well-known midlife crisis when the problem of undevelopment peaks. Which view is correct? Not only can no one say, but we are wise to wonder if our psychological theoreticians are at all astute in their understanding of the human condition.

In his book *Is There a Science of Behavior*, George Von Hilsheimer observed:

> A monumental examination of 2,300 studies found only 19 reports of psychotherapy which used controls, and half of the studies using controls do not favor psychotherapy. Goldstein and Dean edited a collection of investigations which clearly conclude that dynamic, insight-seeking, long term, and verbal therapies are useless if not harmful. Bergin pointed out that two of the studies showed that

some therapists' personalities and experiences proved useful in
therapy but their training, the setting of the therapy, and their techniques were irrelevant. The only significant therapist variable Lohrenz
reported as significantly affecting the success of therapy with college
students was the therapists' familiarity with campus slang!

Consider how psychoanalysts have tackled the "case" of Vincent
van Gogh. In *The Psychoanalyst and the Artist*, Daniel Schneider had
this to say about van Gogh:

Van Gogh lives under the constant overpowering threat and
masochistic passive homosexual unconscious wish for castration. His
relationship to Paul Gauguin, who is as sadistic as Vincent is
masochistic, is an epitome of this violent conflict between love of men
and hate-filled disappointment in them—a conflict terminating in an
abortive attack on Gauguin with a razor when Gauguin comes to live
with Vincent in the "yellow house" in Arles. Instead he amputates his
ear and sends the bloody mess to a prostitute who has praised his ears
for their pinkness—and yet, unforgivably accepted Gauguin. How
thinly disguised is his terrifying, physical love for the sadistic Paul!

If you have a taste for this sort of thing, you might exclaim,
"Bravo! Of course van Gogh's antics during Gauguin's visit are about
sadism and masochism, latent homosexuality, and so on." But if this
is correct, why do other psychoanalysts provide entirely different explanations for Vincent's behavior? In *Portraits of the Artist*, John Gedo
argues that van Gogh's dramas with Gauguin are related to his enduring "merger fantasy," a fantasy most clearly shown in his relationship with his brother Theo. This "merger fantasy" is related to
van Gogh's "martyr complex" and to the organization of his religious
thinking. Gedo wrote:

Vincent apparently experienced Gauguin's presence in Arles
in 1888 as an expansion of the symbiotic system with Theo. In

circumstances of this kind, struggles for dominance within the collective are unavoidable. Their occurrence here is most clearly revealed in Van Gogh's temporary acceptance of Gauguin's method of working from the imagination, and Vincent indeed produced several paintings heavily influenced by the French artist's style. We may infer that the symbiotic pull was equally strong in the opposite direction from the crudity of Gauguin's later boast that at Arles he had taught Van Gogh the most valuable aspects of his art. We may glimpse the profound significance of Van Gogh's merger fantasies at the time if we think of his self-mutilation in response to Gauguin's determination to leave him as a symbolic expression of his feeling that he was about to lose a part of himself.

In the best-known psychoanalytic biography of van Gogh, Albert Lubin's *Stranger on the Earth*, Lubin explained:

Vincent is a good example of this relationship between depression and masochism. He took the suffering of depression and, instead of being crushed by it, glorified it—first in the name of Christ and then in the name of art. He exhibited it to his parents, his brother, and to all the world. He swung back and forth between paralyzing depressive states of relatively short duration and productive masochistic-creative states. In his identification with the crucified Jesus, the masochistic use of depression enabled him to accept unhappiness as a means of obtaining the approbation of his fellow man as well as eternal joy in heaven. With the glorification of suffering, the thought of suffering remained but the feeling diminished. He appeared to accept the cruel demands of the rejecting, punishing, shaming world by rejecting, punishing, and shaming himself; but, at the same time, he rejected this world and asserted his intimacy with God and heaven. He made a compact with the sadists, but he also defied them. By becoming a martyred hero, he turned guilt into innocence and shame into pride.

Is van Gogh's depression related to his latent homosexuality, his merger fantasy, his martyr complex, his anger at his mother, his anger at his father, his anger at Jesus, his love of Jesus, his glorification of suffering for its own sake, his glorification of suffering as a defense, or what? I think it is fair to say that these retrospective diagnoses are really more insults than insights. It should be clear why psychodynamic approaches to the treatment of depression have the worst outcome rates. According to recent studies, psychodynamic approaches had a 34 percent success rate, as opposed to 55 percent for behavioral treatment, 52 percent for interpersonal treatment, and 50 percent for cognitive treatment.

ADDED VULNERABILITIES

I believe that depression in creative individuals is best thought of as a meaning crisis caused by chronic, persistent uneasiness, irritation, anger, and sadness about the facts of existence and life's apparent lack of meaning. Anyone who examines the facts of existence and strives to find personal meaning, as creative people do, opens herself up to this depression. But another group of people are also vulnerable to these same meaning crises, a group among whom many creative people will number themselves. These are our harmed children, now grown up, who have endured structural changes because of unfortunate childhood experiences.

We have interesting evidence, drawn from the rat and monkey worlds, about the actual structural changes you can effect on the brain by abandoning, neglecting, or abusing an infant. If you harm an infant rat or monkey in certain ways, you not only produce immediate responses but you also produce structural brain changes that last a lifetime. Their neurons change, the way they secrete hormones changes, their biology changes.

Likewise, the child who is harmed is likely to become biologically altered in such a way that life becomes dark and meaning crises loom everywhere. This infant grows into an adult with a toxic brain structure, neurons at the ready to overreact to stress and to see the glass not as half-empty but as completely empty and impossible to fill. You can't say that a structural anomaly or hormonal irregularity you observe in a depressed person is genetic, since it was just as likely caused by her parents informing her that she was going to hell or treating her like she was in hell already.

Charles Nemeroff explained in "The Neurobiology of Depression":

> We conducted a series of experiments in which neonatal rats were neglected. We removed them from their mothers for brief periods on about 10 of their first 21 days of life, before allowing them to grow up (after weaning) in a standard rat colony. As adults, these maternally deprived rats showed clear signs of changes in CRF [corticotropin-releasing factor]-containing neurons all in the direction observed in depressed patients—such as rises in stress-induced ACTH [adrenocorticotropic hormone] secretion and elevations of CRF concentrations in several areas of the brain. Levels of corticosterone [the rat's cortisol] also rose. These findings suggest that a permanent increase in CRF gene expression and thus in CRF production occurred in the maternally deprived rats.

Nemeroff continued:

> Studies of Bonnet macaque monkeys, which as primates more closely resemble humans, yielded similar results. Newborns and their mothers encountered three foraging conditions for three months after the babies' birth: a plentiful, a scarce, and a variable food supply. The variable situation evoked considerable anxiety in monkey mothers, who became so anxious and preoccupied that they basically ignored their offspring. As our model predicts, the neonates in the variable-foraging condition were less active, withdrew from in-

teractions with other monkeys, and froze in novel situations. In adulthood, they also exhibited marked elevations of CRF concentrations in spinal fluid.

You do not need any particular genetic predisposition for these structural changes to occur. All you need is to have been neglected, abandoned, or otherwise traumatized. While we have all been traumatized to some extent, a significant number of people have been traumatized to the extent that real biological change has occurred and made them more susceptible to meaning crises. Since harmful experiences in childhood can cause biological changes, such that neurons change their shape and hormones are expressed in new ways, when you observe such effects in the adult you can't posit a genetic cause. What you are seeing is as likely nurture as nature. Nor are you entitled to offer a psychological explanation, not when the root cause is an interaction between the facts of existence, experienced as stressors, and a brain rebuilt by childhood experience to react negatively to stressors.

A creative person is vulnerable to meaning crises, and hence depression, by virtue of her relationship to meaning. She will have significant added vulnerabilities if she was harmed in childhood—if she was molested, like Virginia Woolf; raised in a frigid religious environment, like van Gogh; witness to the murder of his father, like Dostoyevsky. As we look at the steps necessary to maintain meaning and reduce depression, we will have to provide additional strategies that take into account the harm that many creative people have experienced.

1

TWO MEANING
CASUALTIES

Meaning is our territory, and casualties on the battlefield of meaning are our subjects. Depression in creative people is essentially a meaning problem and must be handled by a meaning expert: you. Right now you may not consider yourself a meaning expert or even understand the phrase. But as you read along, you will come to understand what a meaning expert is, what she does, and why you must become one.

To be more accurate about it, you will want to become a meta-meaning expert. Your job isn't to find one particular meaning and adopt it as your way of life but rather to learn about the vagaries of meaning, about how meaning comes and goes, about what sustains meaning, and why meaning sometimes vanishes. Then, when you feel yourself becoming depressed, you will know to say, "Must be a meaning crisis!" You will know what to do next to plug up the hole through which meaning is escaping. Even the greatest meaning expert can't keep meaning from leaking out and draining away, but you can learn how to restore meaning and recover from meaning crises.

23

A rocket engineer builds rockets and out of self-interest is obliged to say, "Space travel is good." He has no vested interest in stepping back and thinking about the pros and cons of space travel. Likewise, a minister has a vested interest in saying, "My religion is the true religion." A therapist has a vested interest in diagnosing and treating according to the nostrums of his profession. Most people are invested in a single point of view and find it much too troubling and troublesome to step back, take the "meta" position, and ask, "What is really going on?"

You must take this meta position with respect to meaning if you are to understand your episodes of depression and craft a life you deem worth living. If you don't become a meta-meaning expert, you will find yourself unhappy, regularly uncreative and unproductive, and sometimes even suicidal. Your two eyes are not enough—you must cultivate a third idea with which you monitor the ebb and flow of meaning in your life. Just as you can't sense the fact that billions of neutrinos are passing through your body as you read this passage, most people can't sense that they are engaged in a never-ending interplay with meaning.

This will be new territory for most of you. Probably you've studied a little psychology, philosophy, religion, and other disciplines that claim meaning as their subject matter. But none of these fields demands that you come to your own conclusions about what meaning means. I believe that you need to do exactly that, that the crux of the matter is articulating what life will mean for you and how you will keep personal meaning alive in the face of repeated meaning crises. We will have to use language in new ways because no common vocabulary of meaning currently exists. We will also need to think in new ways, as if we were brilliant babes in the woods looking at life for the first time.

Let me preview what answers won't work. It will not work to say, "If I manage to create, that will be enough meaning for me." It will not work to say, "If I divine what the universe wants of me and if I obey its commands, that will constitute my meaning." It will not work to say, "If I lose my mind, that may bring some peace." It will not work to say, "If I blend in and accept the meanings of my culture, that ought to work for me, since it appears to work for other people." It will not work to say, "Maybe I can revisit some former meaning, say my birth religion or that philosophy I dabbled in when I was 19, and fully embrace that received wisdom." These familiar answers will not work. To understand why, we need to investigate what meaning means to a contemporary human being, to someone who knows too much to make do with old answers but who hasn't stretched into the skin she needs to wear: the skin of a heroic meaning-maker.

HOW A BEST-SELLER PRECIPITATED A MEANING CRISIS

Consider Barry. Barry is 37, was married for a few years and currently lives alone, has at times smoked a lot of marijuana, and for more than a decade marginally survived on the interest from savings left to him by his parents. In his 20s, Barry wrote three novels that were never published. Then, at 34, he had a novel published that became a best-seller. His life changed: He became seriously depressed.

He spent the year after the publication of his novel publicizing it and gearing up to write its sequel. But no sequel visited him. Serious and self-respectful enough to know not to embark on a meaningless new novel just because he was a hot commodity, he nevertheless felt intense pressure to come up with a sequel and to "strike while the iron was hot." But a year passed and then another without a good idea for a novel arriving.

Barry had been periodically depressed before his best-seller but now found himself suffering from the worst depression of his life, one that was practically paralyzing. To the casual outsider, including an unwary therapist, it looked like Barry must be having psychological problems. Did he "fear success"? Was some sinister Oedipal dynamic playing itself out where Barry felt like he had "murdered his father" and was now "sleeping with his mother"? Did his success and the subsequent strain for an "even bigger" hit trigger a latent biochemical major depression? These are a few of the reasons Barry would have heard proffered by professionals as to why he was seriously depressed when, by all rights, he should have been happily writing his sequel.

The fact of the matter is that Barry finds himself in the grip of a profound meaning crisis precipitated by two events: writing a best-seller and struggling with his best-seller's sequel. It is a meaning crisis on several scores. First, as long as Barry possesses no idea for his sequel, he is bereft of meaning. He can go through the motions of living, he can order Chinese food, chat at the café with acquaintances, watch the evening news, and so on, but the absence of an idea for his sequel is the defining fact of his existence. He "ought to be writing his sequel," but no sequel is there yet, and its absence is a meaning killer.

He can force something out and manage to write each day, and indeed on some days he does exactly that, starting one novel, writing a few pages, then abandoning it. But these false starts and appropriate stops wear him out. Rather than providing him with occasional meaning—meaning for a day, as it were—they underscore the fact that no meaning currently attaches to his life. He is aware that his ideas for a sequel are second-rate and that he is writing just to be doing something, which makes the experience of writing meaningless.

Second, he has learned the impressive, disconcerting lesson that having a novel published and soaring to the top of the best-seller lists does not settle any meaning questions. All his life, up to the point of his success, he supposed that something would change with success.

He wasn't naive enough to imagine that life would become a bed of roses, but he supposed that with success would come some ease. Then he would be able to exorcise a few demons and feel better about himself and the facts of existence. In short, he imagined that writing a best-seller would prove a positive existential landmark.

Exactly the opposite happened. He found that his meaning problems doubled or tripled, not halved. With success came a new, deeper doubt that any activity, even his cherished writing, could make life mean anything. From this dark doubt flowed an inability to feel pleasure, which he now suffered from for the first time in his life. Previously, writing gave him pleasure, revising gave him pleasure, many aspects of his life gave him pleasure. Now nothing gives him pleasure, not fan letters, accolades, and certainly not his writing, which is currently "all wrong." His success, which he had dreamed of but the reality of which is a meager thing, has produced the bizarre result of removing all pleasure from his life.

Barry's meaning crisis has many facets. First, he possesses no current meaning while he waits for a sequel to make itself known to him. Second, he has learned the terrible lesson that his meaning problems will not end with success and instead have taken on a new, implacable face. Third, the very nature of meaning appears to have changed. The good meaning he had hoped to make and which he perhaps did make in his successful novel is no longer enough. Now, with expectations on him that he write at the same level or higher, he is obliged to make "even greater meaning." The meaning bar has shifted higher, and he faces his personal variation of the question Tolstoy had to answer and never could: "What is an adequate sequel to *War and Peace*?"

What was previously meaningful, to simply write, no longer is. Now he can only think of the activity of writing as "writing for the critics," "writing for posterity," "writing impressively," "writing an important sequel," "writing mistake-free and mess-free," "writing for his many fans," and so on. Before, the act of creation made sufficient sense. Now, only the act of creating something worthy and wanted makes sense, which is such a change in his meaning field that no sentence he writes, however fine or refined, passes muster. He requires a sequel in order for meaning to be restored but, ironically, he has less chance than before of writing well, now that his meaning field has been drastically altered by success.

Fourth, he finds himself attacked by waves of guilt and doubt about the path he has chosen to travel, that of an isolated, alienated writer. Previously, his path and his creed made sense: "I am a witness, a truth-teller, an artist." He could forgive himself his failures at relationships and his shortfalls as a person by arguing that his art had to come first, that he was destined to write and was put on earth to create, not to relate. Now that formulation makes less sense since he sees exactly what success means, does, and brings. Perhaps he should have lived differently, loved more, tried harder to make friends and be a friend. Thoughts of this sort now plague Barry.

What could be odder than to have no doubt while having no success and then tremendous doubt as soon as a great success hits? How upside-down that sounds! Yet isn't the experienced cleric more prone to doubt than the seminary student, the experienced therapist more prone to doubt than the intern, the experienced professional in any field more prone to despair and meaning loss than the innocent who still believes? This is Barry's situation. Now he knows about publicists, interviewers, regional marketing managers, and everything else that exists behind the veil. This knowledge brings with it a giant doubt about the true value of his path.

Fifth, and worst of all, his enjoyment of time has changed. Before, when he finished writing for the day, and even if what he produced was poor or skimpy, he could move on to the rest of his day and find meaning in his other activities. He could read a novel, sit in a café, get excited about a woman. The hour he spent over a beer in his local café was fine, full of the simple meaning that human beings experience when they sit among their fellow human beings in cafés. Formerly, that hour constituted no meaning problem, even though he was not actively making meaning.

Now he can hardly sit still. Suddenly—and horribly—what used to feel fine as a way of passing the time between episodes of real meaning-making now feels meaningless. Since he is not writing, since he is not sure that he wants to write, and since he no longer knows what path he ought to follow, all his seconds are colored by his discontent and malaise. His meaning problems have made him manic. He finds himself in a strange rush, pressured to get from the café back to his apartment, pressured, as soon as he gets back to his apartment, to go out again.

This restlessness, as he runs from one place to the next, looking for meaning but experiencing only a meaning vacuum, continues while he sleeps. Barry has become insomniac. To a therapist, his insomnia is a classic symptom of his depression. To a meaning expert, his insomnia is the natural result of his current meaning crisis, as the anxiety of meaning gone missing pesters him day and night and prevents him from resting. Though insomniac, he also sleeps for long stretches during the day. Sometimes he dozes off at 10:00 in the morning and sleeps until 4:00 in the afternoon. To a therapist, this is another symptom of depression. To a meaning expert, dozing off in the middle of the afternoon is an escape from the experience of meaninglessness.

Of course Barry is depressed. If he visits a therapist, however, he will not be asked about his meaning problems. He may be asked to talk about his childhood. He may be told that he needs a medical consultation and may soon find himself on antidepressant medication. A behavioral therapist may pinpoint as the problem the fact that Barry isn't writing much and may help Barry articulate a writing plan. Barry may be told to write such-and-so-many words a day or spend such-and-so-many minutes in front of his computer. A relationship thera-

pist might focus on the lack of intimacy in Barry's life and discuss with
him how he might meet someone and fall in love. Literally not one of
them will say, "How has the meaning in your life changed recently,
and what do you suppose these meaning changes signify?"

What if Barry tells his therapist the following very clear thing?
"There can be no meaning in my life until a good sequel to my successful novel makes itself known to me, plus I no longer believe that
I will ever settle the meaning issues in my life, plus the very nature of
meaning has changed by virtue of my success, plus my enjoyment of
time away from writing has altered dramatically, plus many more
meaning problems than just these are currently plaguing me." The av-
erage helping professional will shrug her shoulders in response, not
knowing what to do with this information.

Not knowing what to do with it, she will ignore Barry's understanding of his situation and reply with some variation of the following dodge: "Yes, that may be true, but I still believe that we should
focus on 'X.'" "X" may be the possibility that Barry has a biochemical imbalance, is unconsciously raging against his dead parents, is
too isolated and alienated for his own good, and so on. The helping
professional—psychotherapist, psychiatrist, herbalist, cleric, social
worker, counselor—will return Barry to the territory with which she
is most familiar.

In fact, Barry may agree to be redirected. He may let go of his formulation of the problem and agree with his therapist's reframe, as
any one of the things that she says may be true and because they connect to the fourth facet of his meaning crisis, that he has been neglecting aspects of his life for the sake of his art and that those
neglected aspects probably need addressing. He may say, "All right,
doctor, if you say so." Indeed, it may ultimately help him to work on
relationship issues or to ventilate simmering resentments about his
childhood. This work may lead to a partial meaning restoration and
may help Barry feel less depressed, as he ingests chemicals or tries to

lead a less-isolated life. His therapist may be able to chalk Barry up as a success, and Barry may feel better by having focused on what his therapist chose to address.

These gains are likely to be short-lived, however, because Barry has not done the work that would allow him to understand the ebb and flow of meaning in his life. He is not much better prepared than before to understand what his writing can and can't mean, what an intimate relationship can and can't mean, what further success or future failure can and can't mean. He is not only a depression-waiting-to-happen (all creative people remain that, no matter how expert they become at understanding meaning) but he is also opaque to himself and therefore more prone to bouts of depression than he would be if he studied his own meaning field.

The situation I've been describing is utterly typical: A creative person is confronted by meaning problems that escalate into a meaning crisis and precipitate depression. As typical as this situation is, however, it hasn't been named or examined before. Standard procedure is to deem Barry ill. He has mental problems, the disease of depression, and so on. Some years back, the first label to tack on Barry would have been "neurotic." Today, the first line of naming is to call Barry "a patient suffering from the treatable medical illness of depression." Although antidepressants, the treatment for the latter, are demonstrably more effective than psychotherapy, the treatment for the former, the naming is no improvement at all since it continues to obscure what is really happening.

BETTY TRIES TO CREATE MEANING

Let's consider a second example.

Betty lives in the South, where she weaves. She is the mother of three girls, a Catholic who no longer attends church, college educated, and married to a man whom she characterizes as good and decent but not understanding of her need to make art. She has dealt with her regular depressions medically, therapeutically, and spiritually, but some core depression will not go away.

She has characterized this core depression in many different ways. Sometimes she connects it to a painful childhood and to self-esteem issues. Sometimes she connects it to a certain lovelessness in her marriage and in her life. Sometimes she connects it to a felt lack of spirituality. Sometimes she connects it to the difficulties of making art, valuing her art, and selling her art. Each of these reasons makes some sense to her, but none has any real vivacity. They are probably implicated or involved, but are they causal? She doubts that they are.

Betty is unaware that she has meaning problems. She is plagued, however, by an insufficiency of meaning that cuts across everything she thinks, feels, and does. She loves her children, enjoys them, and cherishes them, but they do not make for sufficient meaning in her life. She knows that they will go off and live their own lives, and she will be left with the hole she feels. Nor can her husband fill that hole. Sometimes she feels that her art can completely fill that hole, but she weaves much less regularly than she would like, is happy with only a fraction of her products, and hates going to craft shows and peddling her wares. The thought repeatedly returns to her that art may be the complete answer but that perhaps weaving isn't the right medium, so she has tried her hand at watercolors, poetry, scrapbooking, collage, journaling, even square dance calling and country fiddling.

Despite all that she understands about her situation, Betty does not realize that meaning is the issue. If she had to pick one thing to name as the culprit, she would name her personality. She dislikes her personality. She takes her gardening, for instance, as a good example of her troubles with her personality. She would love to just enjoy her garden. Instead, on some days she looks at her garden with a cool, practical eye, making necessary but joyless calculations about what tree needs pruning or what shrub needs replanting. This side of herself she disparagingly calls "Betty the petty realist." On other days she approaches her garden critically, seeing nothing but weeds and disaster. This side of herself she calls "Betty the worry wart" or "gloomy Betty." She would love her garden to sometimes be just a pleasant place to visit, but her own personality stands in the way.

Whenever Betty thinks about getting some help for her depression, she can only conjure up the usual suspects. A spiritual advisor would suggest that she strengthen her relationship to the divine. A psychic, tarot reader, or astrologer would read the universe's mind. A marriage counselor would want to investigate whether her marriage was working; but Betty already knows the extent to which her marriage is and isn't working. Her girlfriends would half-jokingly, half-seriously suggest that she have an affair. A psychiatrist would suggest an antidepressant. A therapist would want to dredge up her childhood experiences, examine the contents of her thoughts and feelings, and angle for personality change. Her art buddies would complain about the difficulties of making art and of selling art.

Each of these usual suspects would be selling something that Betty has bought before and is not inclined to buy again. It is to a therapist that she especially doesn't care to return. Were she to admit to him that she feels hopeless, worthless, helpless, joyless, fatigued, confused, anxious, sad, and angry, he would be overjoyed to be handed every "symptom of depression" he could possibly want. He would instantly diagnose Betty as depressed. But of course she is depressed! She knows that she is depressed, and that diagnosis adds nothing to her understanding of her situation.

What if Betty were to go to a meaning expert, presuming that she could find one? She would have a different conversation there. He would listen to her presentation and reply, "You know, the task of making meaning rests squarely on your shoulders."

"Meaning what?" Betty might reply.

"That you haven't come to grips with what you intend your life to mean. Until you do, your depression can't lift."

"How am I supposed to know what life means? Nobody really knows."

"Not what life means. What you intend *your* life to mean. You must stop everything and decide on the purpose of your life. Once you've articulated your personal creed, you put it into action. You force life to mean what you intend it to mean. Then, for example, when you find yourself hating your current weaving, you know to say to yourself, 'I'm a having a meaning problem, not a weaving problem. Weaving is meaningful, and I won't change my mind about that just because I'm feeling frustrated. I won't allow this to escalate into a full-blown meaning crisis!' Or if your husband says something that bores you, you know to say to yourself, 'Jim is not able to provide sufficient meaning in my life. But I know that already, and I am the provider of my meaning. So I am not going to get down on him or down on my-self and turn his boring remark into a meaning crisis.' In short, you learn to recognize how every second of your life has a meaning face to it, the face you put on it. Are you following?"

"I am."

"That's the work."

"I think I understand. But you left a big thing out."

"What's that?"

"God."

"You factor God in. When you sit down and analyze your beliefs, you factor in your beliefs about gods. A belief in a god is not an an-swer, only a starting point. Everything remains up for grabs in the meaning realm until you decide where meaning resides and what your life will mean. Even after you make a decision, nothing will be settled. You will have to make new, updated meaning as you learn from your experiences and as your circumstances change."

If Barry and Betty can become their own meaning experts, if they can accomplish the rare thing of articulating how they intend to sustain meaning in the face of meaning crises, they have a chance to manage their depression. If they can overcome the emotional blocks to this examination, if they can come up with a personal creed that they find believable, and if they can learn to recognize how every second either supports or endangers the meaning they intend to make, they have a decent chance of living a life that feels meaningful to them.

2

REFLECTING
ON MEANING

Barry's initial task is to recognize that a meaning crisis is precipitating his depression and that he has the job of actively working at meaning restoration. He already knows that he must work at meaning restoration in some way other than by forcing a sequel into existence since forcing a particular book to exist before it is ready appears impossible. Therefore, a reasonable first question for Barry to ask himself is, "How can I make some meaning while I wait for the meaning of my sequel to arrive?" If Barry is willing to think about this question, he will see that he is not looking for a short answer like "Just do it!" but rather a full conversation about meaning.

Not only does he have to figure out where to invest meaning while he waits for the arrival of his sequel but he also has to determine how life can be made to feel meaningful now that his primary meaning mode, writing, has become a leaky vessel. This is one terrific problem. Additional meaning containers into which he might pour new meaning are not yet in place, which is a second terrific problem. As to how many other meaning problems also exist, only Barry, chatting with himself in this strange territory, can calculate.

This conversation is anything but pleasant and Barry may want to avoid undertaking it. Most people hate thinking about meaning or conversing with themselves about meaning. But there is no other way to arrive at self-awareness. Once meaning problems exist, there is nothing to do but address them. A "good book" will not provide Barry with answers about what his life should mean. Neither a secular book like this one nor a religious book will ultimately impress him since he doesn't put stock in received wisdom. A postmodern agnostic, Barry doubts that people are doing anything but spinning illusions when they announce that this, that, or the other thing is the essential truth. His own belief system has been essentially an inarticulate humanism, and he has to wonder whether that humanism will hold water if he shines a light on it. Quite possibly it won't, which is precisely the fear that prevents Barry from launching into a conversation about meaning.

The fear, simply put, is that if he investigates meaning, he will be forced to recognize that meaning does not exist. He will be forced to conclude that all meanings are illusions and that there are no compelling reasons to do anything. He is afraid that he will discover that he has pushed himself up against what Albert Camus deemed the only question of real interest to a contemporary person: "Why not commit suicide?" Barry fears that any conversation about meaning will bring him either to a dangerous place (utter meaninglessness) or a wicked place (to a belief system he concocts that is a rationalization). He fears the first destination and loathes the second. If he could picture a third destination, he might make the trip.

Betty, for her part, is a believer. Because she believes in a god or a spiritual universe, she may have an easier task than Barry—or she may have a harder task. If there is a god or spiritual universe of the sort she believes in, if she can make sense of how to live in relation to real spiritual laws, and if living in relation to such laws doesn't vio-late her own principles—which they shouldn't, presumably, but who can say?—then she will find comfort in her beliefs and sustainable meaning. In this scenario, she will have an easier time of it than Barry.

By the same token, if there is no God or spiritual universe of the sort Betty believes in but she cobbles together a belief system that, de-spite her claims of belief in God, really rests on a set of cherished principles that hold meaning for her—if, say, she believes in truth, beauty, and goodness but feels compelled to call that triumvirate "God"—she will have created a powerful functional illusion for her-self. She will probably have a much easier time of it than Barry will, so long as she doesn't doubt her own beliefs and puncture her own illusions. If there is a god and Betty can align with that entity, or if there is no god but a god-illusion helps Betty make and maintain meaning and she never comes to doubt her invention, then she is likely to be able to arrive at a creed that will sustain her.

But it is unlikely that any modern person can avoid doubt. By doubting, Betty may dismiss a reality, the actual existence of gods, or puncture a functional illusion and suddenly suspect that the useful gods she previously believed in are just inventions. In either case, she will end up where any unbeliever ends up, not knowing what to believe. This result is typical and naturally causes meaning crises, but it still is a better result than another very typical outcome, where a believer denies her doubts and refuses to reflect on meaning for fear that she will learn something she dreads discovering. If Betty denies her doubts, which in fact has been her consistent pattern, she will be prevented from making meaning and will be left with a never-ending case of the blues. Doubt alone makes meaning-making difficult, but denial of doubt when one actually doubts makes it im-possible.

This denial of doubt may have been van Gogh's precise problem and predicament. He loved Christianity enough to choose preaching the Gospel as his first profession, and had he not been fired from the pulpit for preaching radical ideas about love and brotherhood—ideas that his flock and his superiors found unacceptable—he might have gone on making meaning in that fashion. But the question is, could he have really? Did he believe seamlessly or did he doubt and deny his doubt? Van Gogh often sounds like Alyosha, the innocent believer in Dostoyevsky's *The Brothers Karamazov*, but acts more like Ivan, Dostoyevsky's fevered unbeliever.

At 30, van Gogh wrote to his brother Theo:

> That God of the clergymen, He is for me as dead as a doornail. But am I an atheist for all that? The clergymen consider me as such—be it so; but still there is something mysterious in life. Now call that God, or human nature or whatever you like, but there is something which I cannot define systematically, though it is very much alive and very real, that is God, or as good as God.

Van Gogh's phrase "as good as God" is as significant as Barton's phrase "as lives go" in Barton's suicide note. That something exists which is "as good as God" is not at all the same state of affairs as something existing that is God. Van Gogh never wills himself to examine his doubts, restricting himself instead to a bitter indictment of religion. A few months after the previous letter, he confided to Theo:

> At Christmas I had a violent scene with Father, and it went so far that Father told me I had better leave the house. Well, he said it so decidedly that I actually left the same day. The reason was that I did not go to church, and I also said that if I was forced to go, I certainly should never go again out of consideration, as I had done rather regularly all the time I was in Etten. I told him that I thought their whole system of religion horrible, and just because during a miserable time in my life I had gone so far into those questions, I did not want to think of them any more.

Unfortunately, he needed to think about exactly those questions. Like every contemporary person, van Gogh needed to choose a camp, according to his best understanding of the universe, and work out the conclusions of his choice so that he might truly know what he intended to force his life to mean. If you believe in gods, that must mean something. If you do not believe in gods, that must mean something. If you do not know, one way or the other, but have leanings, that must mean something. If you do not know, one way or the other, and have no clue, that must mean something. To deny that you have something to work out is a path to depression.

Whose meaning tasks are harder: those of the unbeliever who finds the universe meaningless or those of the believer who doubts but clings to belief? Who can say? What we know is that both have grave meaning problems, as evidenced by clerics turning to atheism on their deathbeds and atheists asking for church funerals as their final requests. Both Barry and Betty are in this together, the one hating the idol-making tricks of human beings but recoiling at the emptiness left after the god-ideas have been exorcised, the other experiencing some feeling she wants to call spirit but not knowing what it really signifies or whether she ought to trust it.

What is clear is that neither the modern believer nor the modern unbeliever is excited to have this meaning conversation. Both suspect that they will end up discouraged and doubly depressed, at a place of more doubt and less understanding. Maybe meaning will even go missing entirely. No one has expressed the terror of meaning-gone-missing more eloquently than the playwright Eugene Ionesco, who described his struggles in *Fragments of a Journal*:

> *Which is the right way? Indifference, perhaps. That's not possible; since we are here, we can't help participating; we can't be detached from the manifest world since we are immersed in it. We*

cannot reject the world. Then let's take everything seriously; that's
equally ridiculous. Or can I be like a tree: but I'm not a tree. Or can
I follow the drift of history, in the direction of cosmic evolution?
But nobody knows quite what that means. I don't know the basic
elements of the game. One ought at least to feel at ease; I cannot,
because living is the source of my unease. Anxiety is ignorance. Non-
anxiety is also ignorance. I seem to be going around in a circle. Perhaps I'm not going around in a circle. Perhaps there is no circle. I
cannot laugh, nor weep, nor sit down, nor lie down, nor get up, nor
desire, nor not desire. I am paralyzed.

This is the conversation about meaning that contemporary people
fear they will have and expect they will have once they admit that
meaning is a problem. They recognize that, like Ionesco, they are victims of the righteous demise of blind faith, the installation of ma-
terialism as the world's reigning philosophy, and the widespread
meta-analysis of belief that casts all belief into doubt. They recognize
that they are victims of increased knowledge, increased awareness, and
a paucity of meaning options. To the question, "Why not have a little
conversation about meaning?" they are inclined to answer, "No, thanks!
I know where I'll end up, which is more depressed than I am right now."

FORCING LIFE TO MEAN

We must investigate meaning even though we wish we didn't have to,
even though we pray that meaning would just stay put, and even
though we dream of a time when life might simply mean. The good
news—the great news—is that having this unwanted conversation
about meaning may lead to liberation and not to deeper depression.
What a creative person may learn from her inquiry is that, despite the
fact that she has no choice but to experience pain and suffering, on
the one hand because she is alive and on the other hand because she

is determined to create, she can nevertheless make sense of her time on Earth by deciding to take life seriously.

This option, which Ionesco dismissed as just as ridiculous as any other option, may indeed look ridiculous to the eyes of an indifferent universe, which casts its cold eye on all attempts at meaning-making. But it need not feel ridiculous to any given individual, who can opt independently to take life seriously. This life-affirming conclusion is a bet against the odds, as it were—a bet made ironically, perhaps, but nevertheless made. At the end of this conversation about meaning, the one that she dreaded having, a creative person may smile and declare, "I am opting to matter and to take life seriously."

I am previewing the conclusion that I am recommending. But it is impossible to arrive at this conclusion if your meaning investigation operates as a mere defense against any actual investigation. Some trials are just for show, the verdict a foregone conclusion, and some blue ribbon panels already have their final report written before the evidence is heard. We so dread actually investigating meaning, even when we know that we must, that we can launch into an investigation in which nothing is ventured and nothing is gained. If you investigate meaning defensively, if you do not look reality and your own doubts and dreams squarely in the eye, you will return to the exact spot where you began.

Rollo May, the existential writer, warned that thinking about meaning can—and often does—serve as a defense against really thinking about meaning. He expressed his cautionary note in the following way:

> It must also be added that the tendency to use existential concepts in the service of intellectualizing is especially to be guarded against. The terms, concepts and principles we have discussed can be used as a defense against confronting existential reality, just as readily as any other concepts. Perhaps, because these concepts refer

*to things which have to do with personal reality, they can the more
seductively be used to give the illusion of reality. It helps always to
come back to the existential touchstone of authenticity.*

So it is time to add an adjective to our formulation: You will want
to engage in an *authentic* conversation about meaning, one in which
everything is risked. You risk learning that you must actually listen to
gods or that there are no gods. If you have this conversation, you can
begin to force life to mean. The German novelist Hermann Hesse described the idea of forcing life to mean in the following way:

> *To suppose that man in particular is a whim or cruel game of
> nature is a fallacy that man himself has thought up because he takes
> himself too seriously. Life concerns itself with man no more than
> with the earthworm. We must take the cruelty of life and the inex-
> orability of death into ourselves, not by moaning, but by experi-
> encing our despair to the fullest. Only then, only when we have
> taken all the cruelty or meaninglessness of nature into ourselves,
> can we begin to confront this brutal meaninglessness and force a
> meaning on it.*

OUR STARTING POINT

To heal your depression, you must force life to mean. You force life
to mean by sitting down and deciding what you want your life to
mean. When you are satisfied with your answer, and if you have been
truthful with yourself, you will have stripped away false meanings and
motives and arrived at your best understanding of how you intend to
shape your life. By providing yourself with personal reasons for
taking your own life seriously, you begin to build a shield against
meaninglessness.

These reasons must be personal. The hunt for ultimate reasons will prove a waste of time, even for believers, since we are built to dispute anything, even putative pronouncements from gods. No ultimate reason takes precedence over a righteous human reason for taking action and making meaning. Anaïs Nin echoed this idea when she suggested, "The personal life, deeply lived, becomes universal." If the laws of the universe are not directly within us, where are they? If they are within us, what could make them more purely or more powerfully manifest than living according to our own best reasons for living?

You must tap into your ethical self as well as your egoistic self when you construct your personal creed so that the reasons you arrive at encompass your *principles* as well as your *desires*. Why shouldn't you force life to mean that you get expensive cars and two homes or that you study whatever you like, even if your research harms others? Why become a saint or even a decent person, since it is your decision how you will force life to mean? Because by ignoring your own ethical principles, you are bound to experience the emptiness that comes with denying your conscience.

To find your path, you begin with a core question like one of the following:

- ◆ "How can I force life to have meaning?"
- ◆ "How can I make life feel meaningful to me?"
- ◆ "How can I justify my life?"
- ◆ "What is at the center of a creed I might live by?"
- ◆ "On what operating principles can I base a meaningful life?"
- ◆ "What is my truth?"

Have a fireside chat with yourself with a question of this sort as your starting point. Remember that the question you ask yourself should not be the abstract question, "What is the meaning of life?" In that direction is idle metaphysical speculation. Rather, you create a question that is a variation of "What do I want my life to mean?" or "How do I choose to live?" What you are really asking is the more elaborate question, "Given my limited understanding of the nature of the universe, how shall I organize what I believe to be true into a personal creed that provides me with a sturdy rationale for living?"

Barry, embarking on this conversation, chooses as his starting question, "On what core operating principles can I base a meaningful life?" As he thinks about this question, he is surprised to realize that writing has not actually lost any of its former luster or importance. It is still the place where he intends to make meaning, the place where he can be most human, articulate, and alive. But he sees that he must also force the rest of his life to mean, and he must do so in ways compatible with his core principles. But what are those core principles? The question makes him a little light headed, but he manages to jot down a few notes:

> Generally speaking, it is better to be kind than to be mean.
> I can decide to be good rather than bad.
> I can perhaps be a little helpful, rather than another miserable drag on the universe.
> I can aim to do excellent work, to live my life doing excellent work, even though many projects will fail miserably.
> I can somehow change my minute-by-minute attitude to a more philosophical one, whatever that means exactly.
> I can somehow accept this culture while at the same time refusing to accept it. I can be something like a friendly witness.
> I can be less frightened of meaninglessness and just let it be when it hits, maybe with the ironclad rule that I will only permit two or three hours of meaninglessness before I fight to restore meaning. But what would a fight against meaninglessness look like?

He stops because something odd strikes him. He is feeling calm and not, as he has felt so often recently, manic and hysterical. It occurs to him that he has been fleeing some danger or chasing some elusive salvation ever since his novel became a bestseller. What has this mania been all about? Is it just the expression of his genes, some biological racing that has been causing him to crazily rush from one meaningless thing to the next? He finds it impossible to say. But he senses that this calmness is very different from emptiness, entirely different from the terrible calmness that van Gogh described in the days before his suicide.

Barry has arrived at a starting point. While it is only a starting point, it is a significant moment in any creator's life to quiet his nerves, look questions of meaning in the eye, and begin to articulate a personal creed that will help him negotiate meaning crises. In the ensuing chapters, we'll examine other elements of a creator's plan that combine to armor him in his battle against meaninglessness. But the first task is to stop everything, announce in the mirror to a reluctant self that you are embarking on an investigation of meaning, pose a provocative first question, and stay put as you try to answer your own question.

Betty, for her part, posits a supernatural reality, though how tarot cards, astrology, chi energy, the Taoist way, elements of Catholicism, angels, homeopathy, Jungian psychology, psychic phenomena, and her other beliefs make for a coherent whole is an open question. She also recognizes, however, that she has been depressed many times before, is depressed again, and that her usual answers have proven insufficient. So she wills herself to pose and answer a core question about meaning. She chooses as her question "What is my truth?" and jots down certain words and phrases in response to this question:

Spiritual emergency	*Iconography*
Spiritual necessity	*Children, family*
Simplicity	*Relationships*
Responsibility	*Truth, beauty, goodness*
Courage, not criticism	*Silence*

Reflecting on her list, Betty has the following thought: "I'm not sure I have to articulate a philosophy of life in order to know how to live. I think I can hold each moment up in some intuitive way to a vision I have of what makes for a meaningful life, even though I can't clearly spell out its design. In fact, I think I can let go of some of my need to reproduce that design. I've tried to reproduce that design by weaving mandalas, using symbols from indigenous peoples, and so on, but there's something static and insufficient about that approach. I believe I need to create my own iconography in accordance with this unseen but tangible vision."

Betty has her starting point. To begin with, she will measure her life not against a set of principles but against an intuitive sense of what she wants her life to mean. She will articulate this sense in as few words as possible, in a single phrase or "life plan sentence" that serves as a reminder of her central conclusion—that meaning can be reckoned intuitively on the spot, as she goes about living her life. All she needs to do is pay attention and remember that every moment—whether at her loom, in her garden, with her children, or at a crafts fair—is a potential meaning opportunity.

Now it's your turn, if you like. Calm your nerves a little and begin to engage in self-reflection. Ask yourself a single large question about the meaning of your life: what you want to stand for, what you want to embody, what you want your life to mean. Gingerly and gently, arrive at your real intentions. Discard the easy answers, the ones supplied by your ego, your culture, your parents, your mythology. Discard incomplete answers like "I just need to paint" and "All I need to do is write." The answer you are searching for embodies your principles and your goals and is burning red hot, just beneath the surface of consciousness, like lava beneath the Earth's crust.

If you manage to engage in this self-reflection, you are likely to

notice that your answers begin to separate themselves into three categories: what it means to live a meaningful life, what it means to engage in meaningful work, and what it means to spend time in a
meaningful way. Each of these categories presents its own meaning
problems. Worse, forcing meaning in one category can cause
meaning to leak away in another. We need to examine these added
difficulties as we strive for a true understanding of the task in front
of you: forcing life to mean.

3

MEANINGFUL LIFE, MEANINGFUL WORK, MEANINGFUL DAYS

In order for you to live an authentic, meaningful life, which is the principal remedy for the depression creative people experience, you must feel that 1) the plan of your life is meaningful, 2) the work you do is meaningful, and 3) the way your spend your time is meaningful. These are three separate but related tasks, each with its own logic, demands, and obstacles.

Because these three tasks are truly separate, it is entirely possible to construct a simple life plan that makes meaning sense to you—say, that you will write truthfully and love deeply—as you embark on a difficult writing project that consumes you but that you can't bring to fruition and find that your days feel meaningless because your creative efforts are failing and your intimate life is on hold. In this scenario, your life plan feels meaningful but your actual work and your actual days do not.

Conversely, an earthquake may strike your city and cause a great catastrophe that forces you to let go of your life plan and dive into rescue efforts. Oddly, these days are likely to feel more meaningful than your days struggling with your writing did, as helping others carries with it built-in meaning. In this scenario, your days feel meaningful, but at night you will be struck by the feeling that you are "merely" living since you are not doing your chosen work or living according to your life plan.

All sorts of permutations and combinations of these three tasks are possible. The ideal combination, of course, is that your life plan feels meaningful to you and you actually live it; that the work you've chosen to do feels meaningful to you and you actually do it; and that your days, spent primarily doing your work and living your life plan, feel filled with meaning. To reach this goal, you must consciously hold the following four intentions:

1. To articulate a life plan that feels meaningful and to strive to live by that plan.

2. To articulate what constitutes worthy work and to accomplish that worthy work.

3. To articulate how the seconds, hours, weeks, and years that make up your life will be made to feel meaningful and to strive to actually make them feel meaningful.

4. To put the first three intentions into practice in a coordinated way.

THE FIRST INTENTION:
ARTICULATING A LIFE PLAN

The more abstract our life plan, the easier it will be to feel good about it but the harder it will be to know concretely what we are affirming.

The more concrete our life plan, the easier it will be to know what our tasks are but the more likely we are to overwhelm ourselves with tasks and narrow our possibilities.

If my life plan is "to love and to create," I have a strong, affirmative guiding principle that I can easily remember. But I still must flesh it out if it is to have any real meaning. If, conversely, my life plan is "to write an excellent novel every year, selling and promoting each one after it is written, marry and have three children, have lots of friends and make music with them, investigate every subject that piques my interest, and stand up for truth, beauty, and goodness while convincing others that truth, beauty, and goodness are the highest ideals," then I have set out with considerable clarity what I intend to do with my life, but I have also boxed myself into a corner. Now I need not only children, but three children and not only many novels written and published, but one a year and each a success. This specific life plan, with its many hard-to-achieve goals, practically guarantees a regular and maybe even constant upsetness with the facts of existence.

Given that both approaches entail difficulties, which is better to put into place, a short, abstract life plan sentence or a long, detailed one? If you were holding just one intention, to live your life plan, then a detailed life plan would prove necessary. But because you must hold four intentions—to live your life plan, to do worthy work, to make your time feel meaningful, and to coordinate these three tasks—you should create a brief life plan sentence that allows for maximum flexibility and that provides a memorable reminder of your goals on Earth. Then add details and necessary complexity when you flesh out your other intentions.

You want to articulate your life plan in a single sentence that includes a statement about your personal ethics, a statement about realizing your potential, and a statement about relation-

ships. The life plan sentence you craft might sound like one of the
following:

- ◆ "I intend to be a decent person who makes use of his native gifts
and who lives a life full of creative accomplishments and loving relationships."

- ◆ "I intend to stand up for basic principles of fairness and justice
while manifesting my creative potential and relating to others in a
human way."

- ◆ "I intend to write powerfully and truthfully and share my life
with at least one other person."

- ◆ "I intend to devote my life to music while remembering that I'm
a human being before I'm a musician, with other needs and obliga-
tions in addition to music."

- ◆ "I intend to make discoveries in science while honoring the value
of teaching and intimate relationships."

- ◆ "I intend to create powerful sculptures that move people, get my
sculptures into the marketplace, and live an ethical life that makes me
proud."

Creating a sentence of this sort and using it as the actual blue-
print of your life are profoundly important tasks. They help keep you
on track so that when a particular sculpture fails, you can say, "I
made a mess. But I know what I have to do next, which is simply to
try again. I can start now or I can resume tomorrow and do some
other worthy thing for the rest of today, like love or be of service." The
ruination of one sculpture counts for very little in the context of your
firmly held life plan.

Your life plan provides an internal yardstick against which your
current behaviors can be measured. Instead of not knowing in a given
situation whether, say, to speak up or keep silent—whether to tell off
a particular literary agent or hold your peace, whether to march

against a government action or merely shake your head ironically, whether to withdraw your support from a project or shut one eye and accept the moral imperfection of the situation—you remind yourself of your life plan sentence, test the moment against your plan's intent, and intuitively recognize what path to take.

The very existence of your life plan has a deeply calming effect. Just as a believer is calmed by his belief in a supernatural being who is on his side or, if not on his side, at least not indifferent to his existence, a creator is calmed by having something to believe in that he himself has affirmed. His life plan sentence is his announcement that he intends to mean, and while it does not spell out specific meaning intentions, it provides an outline that is no more vague or less momentous than a believer's belief in gods.

THE SECOND INTENTION: ARTICULATING WHAT CONSTITUTES WORTHY WORK

When a person creates, he has many goals in mind. To focus on just two, he wants to do masterful work, and he also wants to do meaningful work. These are not only different goals, but they often stand in opposition. It is possible to master a small corner of a particular intellectual discipline but not find it meaningful to restrict oneself to that corner. It is possible to master a certain painting style but not find it meaningful to endlessly repeat oneself in that style. It is possible to perfect a literary formula and at the same time hate your lack of writing depth. It is possible to create a technology business that makes money and runs beautifully and simultaneously find your product pointless.

The painter Robert Farber, confronted by the reality of his HIV disease, reported in Andrea Vaucher's *Muses from Chaos and Ash*:

> Three years ago I was doing only large abstract work, color fields. It was very impersonal and influenced by landscape. Then I

got tired of all of that; I wanted to change everything around ar-
tistically. In therapy I was exploring the dysfunctionalism of my
family. I decided that I wanted to explore nightmares that were al-
ways part of my experience, a horror I was always drawn to. At the
same time, I wanted to tell the story of what it was like to use drugs
in the seventies and eighties. So I started doing completely different
work, figurative work. I tried to capture not only the horror of that
kind of voracious pleasure seeking but the craziness of it. But in-
termingled with that were also personal demons that I was exor-
cising. This culminated with a major piece that I felt said it all: what
it was like to be on drugs, the downtown scene, the pleasure and
the sex and all the craziness of it.

There is no good way for a creator to answer the question of
whether he should move from abstraction to realism or from realism
to abstraction, from poetry to prose or from prose to poetry, from
collage to film or from film to collage, except by understanding his
meaning intentions and by fathoming what he considers worthy
work. It isn't that he must be able to articulate what constitutes
worthy work, since it is difficult to put our thoughts into words as
clearly and eloquently as Farber does in the preceding passage. But
he needs to cultivate an intuitive sense of what he means by worthy
work and to learn how to measure whether the creative work he
means to tackle meets his own standards.

Is his budding idea for a novel worthy in his own eyes? Are his
scientific pursuits worthy in his own eyes? Is his software product
worthy in his own eyes? First, he must want to know. That is, he must
hold the intention to investigate whether the creative work he un-
dertakes is worthy in his own eyes. Second, he needs to actually know,
to be able to distinguish in his own mind, quite imperfectly but nevertheless in a real way, between worthy and unworthy projects.

The subject of worthy creative work will occupy a later chapter.

The point to remember for now is that it is vitally important that creative people put on the table the fact that they are intending to create worthy work. They can still compose musical comedies, investigate abstract mathematical ideas, paint all-red paintings, or write romances—but only if they consider these activities worthy and approach these activities righteously. By consciously announcing to themselves that they have set the bar high and intend to take their creative lives seriously, endeavoring to do work that is both masterful and meaningful, they take a giant step in the direction of forcing life to mean.

THE THIRD INTENTION: ARTICULATING HOW TIME WILL BE MADE TO FEEL MEANINGFUL

It is a great accomplishment if you manage to put together a personally meaningful life plan and actually live it, and if you learn what constitutes personally meaningful creative work and actually create it. But as much as all that is, it is not enough to ward off meaning crises and bouts of depression. You must also acquire the habit of forcing the seconds, minutes, hours, days, weeks, and months of your life to mean. If you don't, you will experience a confounding emptiness that no amount of righteous living or creative accomplishment can counteract.

You might think, for instance, that it would be possible to create for several hours and then say, "I have made enough meaning for today. Let me just experience the rest of today as 'meaning neutral.'" But this is unlikely to work. One proof of this is the way that creative individuals talk about their time spent not creating. Jackson Pollock observed, "Painting is no problem. The problem is what to do when you're not painting." Tennessee Williams echoed, "Once I finish writing, the rest of the day is posthumous." A creator's time spent not creating can feel like a living death if he hasn't figured out how to force his other time to mean.

If we are living in suspended animation, with time on our hands meaning nothing in particular, we can pass that time by watching television, working at a boring job, giving in to an addiction, and so on, without feeling the despair of meaninglessness. But creative people find this state of suspended animation morally repugnant and psychologically untenable. They do not experience time as something to be happily squandered but as successive chunks that they will either force to mean or carelessly waste.

It is this sense of time as vitally important, a position connected to core principles of personal freedom and responsibility, that causes creators to require time to mean. Time is of the essence. If I have set out to investigate the laws of nature but I am not investigating them, if I have set out to photograph the last wild places but I am not photographing them, if I have set out to turn my memories of my Yiddish grandparents into a musical but I am not writing it, I am violating my own code of ethics.

Creative people pay a severe penalty when they try to live in some kind of "meaning neutral" state. What they would really like to do is keep creating. But they can't because creating is taxing and can only be done for so many hours at a time. Creative individuals feel guilty about not using this other time in the service of their creative work but feel unequal to the task of doing any more creating. Thus, the passage of this other time is experienced as a blemish, a moral flaw, an ignoble defeat.

Even when they are not brooding about wasting time, they are still confronted by the question of what they should do with the time on their hands. The majority of people answer this question by doing customary things for customary reasons. Creative people are not satisfied with such a careless, pointless solution. Instead, they pester themselves about good reasons for taking the next action, the action after that, and the one after that. This self-pestering sounds like a twin to the tormented internal debate we encountered in Ionesco's journal:

> I agree that it might be wise not to burden myself with guilt about time slipping through my fingers. But what should I actually do? Apart from going to the bathroom, sleeping eight hours, and taking care of the other functions of a living organism, what is my agenda? Should I prepare three meals a day because that's some kind of custom, even though I don't need three meals? Should I read the newspaper because people customarily "keep up on the news," even though I'm not interested in what passes for news? Should I volunteer at my child's elementary school, even though it would embarrass him for me to show up there? Should I clean the house, even though a clean house holds no meaning for me? Should I play a lot of golf, which I can rationalize as a form of exercise but which is merely a pastime? Should I bring work home from the office and transform my day job into my whole life? I would rather do things that are meaningful, but what are they?

After this debate has raged for some time, what will a creator end up doing with his other seconds, minutes, and hours? Having arrived at no satisfactory answers, he is likely to surrender, give up on forcing life to mean, and engage in a meaning substitute, something that calms him, numbs him, satisfies him, or feeds his ego. He will have a drink, and then several more. He will look for sex, and then more sex. He will hang out with his buddies for days and weeks at a time. He will fantasize and continue fantasizing.

How can a creative person meaningfully use the seconds, minutes, hours, and days that confront him and not settle for meaning substitutes? In one of three ways. First, he can grant meaning to the bare necessities of life, the time spent sleeping, eating, showering, and

so on. This is not a linguistic game but a carefully considered conclusion based on the premise that to demean that which is necessary
must be an anxiety event or a form of self-sabotaging unfriendliness.

Second, he can invest meaning in the idea, promulgated by many
philosophies and religions, of "being present." Our version of being
present, however, is different from the common variety. Being present for us is an aware state that carries with it the tension of a life
carefully lived. Even when he is engrossed in eating an apple or
watching his child play soccer, he is nevertheless guided by his life
plan and watched over by his third eye, the one that monitors the vagaries of meaning.

In this view, presence is a dance, not a meditation; an engagement, not an emptying. Being present in this improved sense is being
intentionally present for the sake of reasons you deem meaningful.
Every so often you may deem it meaningful to pay complete attention to the cup of tea you are drinking, but more often you will find
yourself drinking your tea while also thinking about your symphony,
chatting with your child, reading the literature of your field, or reflecting on what meaning you want to make next.

Cézanne, painting in the woods, concentrating and taking minutes between brush strokes, was present for the sake of his painting.
A good parent as she listens to her child tell of his school day is present for the sake of her child. A good therapist is present for the sake
of his client. A novelist lost in the trance of writing is present for the
sake of her novel. Pascal, wrestling with a mathematical problem, was
present to reach the right conclusions. In each of these cases, the individual has an intention driving his or her desire to be present, an
intention in the realm of meaning.

Third, he can work on one or another of the core tasks that all
creative people are obliged to tackle. He can decide to use his next
chunk of time creating, even if he isn't quite feeling up to creating.
He can sit back and contemplate his next project. He can practice,

prepare, market, network. He can take some small action in support of his intention not to be an addict. Rather than allow himself to proceed on thoughtless autopilot, he can do one of the things on his long list of meaningful actions, a list that does not exist until he brings it into existence.

THE FOURTH INTENTION: PUTTING THE FIRST THREE INTENTIONS INTO PRACTICE

An aspect of existence that causes creators no end of grief and depression is that their life plans and the ways they spend their time can feel completely at odds. I may feel certain that it is righteous and meaningful to fight for good causes as an environmental lawyer. But I may still experience my days as dreadful as I spend an endless two years unsuccessfully litigating against a multinational corporation. I may sculpt on the side for the sake of my creative life. I may use my creativity in my law practice to make my arguments as persuasive as possible. In small ways I may be able to maintain my sense that life is meaningful. But my days writing briefs, filing motions, waiting for court to convene, and otherwise doing my job, while integral to my life plan, are likely to feel utterly meaningless.

I may know for sure that I must be a singer/songwriter, that music is my medium and the way to fulfill my potential, but hate my days as a waiter and feel my life slipping by as I wait tables and rarely write. In addition, I experience this passage of time as horrible because I have chosen a youth-oriented business that becomes progressively less interested in me as I age. To top it off, because I have stage fright, I spend much of my time in dread of the open mike performances I intend to give. Even though I truly love music, as I haltingly pursue my dream I experience my hours, days, and weeks as pointless, anxiety filled, and unproductive.

If our plan feels meaningful in the abstract but not meaningful in reality, our intentions clash. If our plan feels meaningful only if we experience success and we don't experience sufficient success, our intentions also clash. It is very hard to keep living for future success, to slough off large chunks of time—months, years, even decades—in the hope that one day we will gain some recognition, make some money, and feel fulfilled. How can it feel meaningful in the moment to paint another painting when none of your paintings sell? How can it feel meaningful to go to your corporate job, which you would never have taken except to support your painting life, when you know that your painting life is not succeeding and may never succeed? In such circumstances, your life plan may still make all the sense in the world since painting has not lost its luster, but the reality of your situation makes you despair.

You might try to respond that the act of creation is the meaning reward and that it doesn't matter if you have to spend 60 hours a week at your corporate job or if you never sell a painting. As heroic as this vision is, it is virtually impossible to maintain. Furthermore, creating is not always its own meaning reward. Instead, creating presents its own meaning crises. Creating is not a task like painting the fence or mowing the lawn, the success of which you can pretty much guarantee. It is an enterprise with a substantial chance of failing. This reality further reduces the chance that you can maintain your life plan.

You might spend a year on your first novel and make a hash of it. Except for those rare moments during that year when you wrote some sentences that pleased you, the rest of the time would have passed as something of a perpetual meaning crisis. Every day that the novel went poorly—that is, most days out of that year—you would find yourself asking, "Am I cut out for this?" "Do I have any talent?" "Do I have any idea what I'm doing?" "Who wants this ugly mess?" and "Where's the meaning in this path I've chosen?" You are living your life plan exactly as it should be led, getting your first novel behind you and learning from the experience, but what it feels like in the moment is torture.

It turns out that it is fiendishly hard to carry out the intention of living your life plan, creating worthy work, and making everyday time feel meaningful. Can anybody do this? The only person who has a chance of pulling off what amounts to a miracle is someone who has recognized that the universal silence is primarily punctuated by one sound, the sound of his own thoughts. If his thoughts further defeat him, he has no chance. But if he can enlist his thoughts on his own behalf, then the realization of his intentions becomes a possibility.

4

SOUNDING SILENCE

If we had the consciousness of a cat or a dog, we would have it in us to become perfect Zen masters. We could gnaw on a bone, take a nap, play with a spider until we killed it, get our litter just right, and be innocently and serenely present. Meaning would mean nothing to us, nor would we need it to mean anything. We would be free, and we would be spared. But we are human beings, and we possess that odd duck—human consciousness.

We are able to observe the universe and think about the facts of existence. Very often this observing and thinking leads us to the conclusion that things are wanting. We find our own human nature wanting. We find the universe, which was not designed to serve our needs, wanting. We find our dreams beautiful to contemplate, preposterously hard to realize. Self-interest, competition, envy, and other phenomena sometimes defeat our human relations. Meaning appears suspect or absent.

We start to acquire a negative view of existence in all of its aspects. Our self-talk and inner dialogue begin to take on this negative coloration. We spend more and more time chiding ourselves about something, angry with ourselves about something, upset about something, afraid of something. At the same time, we busily chide others and fill up our minds with resentments, grudges, and dreams of revenge. Between attacking ourselves and attacking others, there is little mind space left for anything productive.

It turns out that we are often engaged in an unfriendly conversation with ourselves or others that causes us pain, subtracts rather than adds meaning, and silences the better conversation we might be having about our creative efforts. We are much more likely to think about our problems than our novel, our enemies than our sculpture, our worries than our interests. Is it any wonder that creative people accomplish so much less than they believe they ought to accomplish and, by all rights, should accomplish? And what if they have acquired an especially bleak worldview because of childhood harm? Then how negative will their self-talk sound?

Cognitive psychology presents a simple model for dealing with the serious problem of negative self-talk. You begin by eavesdropping on yourself and really listening to what you are saying. This is thought identification. If you don't like what you are saying, you exclaim, "I don't want this damned thought!" This is thought confrontation. You banish the negative thought and replace it with a positive, friendlier thought. This is thought substitution. If you master this three-step program, you will have done a tremendous amount to improve your mental health and relieve your depression.

Robert Boice researched the clinical literature in an effort to assess the effectiveness of different methods for treating writers' block and concluded that cognitive therapy produced the best results. He described his own method: to focus on identifying what writer-clients were saying to themselves, to bring the writer's language into awareness, to note which self-statements were distracting or counterproductive, and to build a treatment plan to counter the writer's negative self-talk.

Does this solution go deep and far enough? Certainly not if you are adamant in your desire to hold on to your pain and to find the facts of existence wanting. If both voices in the conversation in your head are the voices of a stubborn, defeated victim in commiseration with himself about the unfairness of life, then cognitive therapy— and every other therapy—will fail. But if one voice is at odds with the other, if one voice speaks for the part of you that wants to recover meaning, then this three-step program is a miracle of simplicity and effectiveness.

IDENTIFYING AND DISPUTING PROBLEMATIC SELF-TALK

If you would actually like to change your mind about the facts of existence and stand in new relationship to them, then the fact that you can dispute your own thoughts turns out to be a great blessing. When you say something to yourself that is unfriendly and a meaning drain, like "I am doing a really stupid job on this chapter," you have the chance to dispute what you just said in the very next breath. Unlike a psychotic, who claims to experience his thoughts as orders that he must obey, you can question what you say, rebuke yourself for demeaning yourself, laugh sardonically at your self-pestering, and otherwise respond to your negative thoughts as they surface.

It is a mistake, leading to a meaning crisis, to not dispute thoughts that do not serve you. If all the paintings you have ever painted are lined up in your garage, unwanted and gathering dust, and as you think about them you think, "Half are garbage, I'll never sell them, painting is meaningless, and I'm an idiot," then in the very next second you are obliged to respond, "No, thank you, I will not entertain you, you despicable thought!" You may also be obliged to plot a new life path and embark on different creative work, but first of all you are obliged to combat this killer thought, which, if allowed to circulate in your brain unchecked, is bound to seriously depress you.

I teach the creativity coaches I train to notice their thoughts and to dispute the problematic ones. Rosemary Warden, a writer and creativity coach, observed:

> In a week like this one, when my "day job" schedule picks up pace and requires more hours than usual, my negative self-talk increases a lot. This week I heard myself thinking:
>
> "Why did I decide to take this technical writing assignment? It's sucking up all my energy so I have no time to work on my creative projects. I must not have been thinking very well to make that decision."
>
> And: "I can't do creative work when I'm working more than eight hours a day."
>
> And: "What's the use trying to learn pen-and-ink drawing? Visual art takes more time than I have to devote to it. It's hard enough to find time to write as it is, without taking on more."
>
> As these thoughts came up, I sometimes countered them with more self-affirmative thoughts like, "I made the best decision I could make at the time, given the circumstances." Or "Even if I'm tired, I can take a half-hour tonight to stay in touch with my creative project by just reading what I've written so far on it." The affirmations help some, but what really helps me most is looking at where the negative self-talk comes from. When I go deeper into it, I begin to see that I may be giving in to the demands of work and relationships too much. I start to wonder whether I could be more of my own self-advocate. I see that perhaps I'm thinking the external world has more power to affect my life than it actually does, or that at least I could respond to the external world differently.

Even deeper down, what I find is an inner stance that gives rise to the negative self-talk in the first place. When I look, I find that I'm abandoning myself and letting external demands outweigh my own needs. Overall, I notice that I appear to be focusing more on what I can't do rather than on what's possible. Once I understand this, I somehow start to feel more free and positive. My plan for myself is to try out a different inner stance—to befriend myself!—and take opportunities to look at what is possible. On the practical level, this means taking time for restoring my energy, creating self-talk that reflects my desire to be my own self-advocate, and breaking down what appear to be large projects into tiny doable bits.

It feels like such a simple yet powerful thing: to go over to my own side rather than to side against myself.

Jori Lynn Walker, poet, painter, and creativity coach, reported:

After weeks of spiraling around within my own project, I've finally emerged, like a woodworm, to a breath of fresh air. I've reached a brand-spanking new starting place—distantly related to the initial concept but richer and much more interesting—and I'm ready to start afresh. And, of course, what do I find? The Voices. "All of your ideas are cliché, why do you even try?" "This is so boring it's not even worth thinking about." "Hey, what about THAT idea?" And so on.

This is an old, familiar place. But this time I'm not letting myself get away with it. I'm on myself like glue and writing like a fiend. I find I've been spontaneously watching every thought and as soon as I get a whiff of sabotage, I'm in my journal taking it apart. So much of what I'm doing right now is changing habits, and to this end, simply changing the thoughts I'm sending myself is immensely helpful.

But at the moment, I'm dealing with a knotty problem in the realm of meaning, and just changing habits isn't going to be enough. In order to go on, I need not only to give myself permission to make the kinds of pictures I want to make, but to truly recognize my love for them. Am I to be a "serious" painter or to do what I love, which is to illustrate? "Drawing pictures" is what I did when I was a kid before I studied painting and became an adult. I can easily imagine that I demean illustration not only because it falls outside the scope of my education but also because it falls outside of what I consider my "adultness." It's just drawing silly pictures, for heaven's sake.

So the self-talk I have to deal with connects to how I want to make meaning. I love illustration and I want to do it, and I have to find a way to wed these two warring factions, "serious" painting and "silly" illustration. I don't want to throw the baby out with the bath water by saying that everything I learned from my painting master is hindering me, so good-bye. There is a huge lesson in my self-talk for me to understand and this is where I am, perched at the moment of bringing together the two most important parts of my artistic self.

Kay Porterfield, a writer and creativity coach, explained:

Throughout the course of my life, I have earned the equivalent of a Ph.D. in negative self-talk, both of the simple and the complex sort. I deal with it by stopping what I am doing and dialoguing with whatever voice is hollering for attention. If I try to ignore it, I continue to work, but the quality of my work suffers, and I become more anxious or depressed as the negative self-talk voice begins screaming for attention.

My steps are to listen to the voice, determine what part of me or whose internalized voice is speaking, and to do a brief written left-hand/right-hand dialog with the voice to find out what it really wants or needs. Usually there is some underlying issue arising and if I ignore it, it persists. This process, which takes 5 to 10 minutes, allows me to see how I can meet the real and often valid need beneath the negative self-talk and continue to do my creative work that day. This might mean writing two pages and then calling a friend or mailing my bills before I sit down at the computer or just

getting out my résumé and reading it over to reassure myself that,
yes, I really have done all that.

I've found that negative self-talk thrives in isolation and even-
tually, when it has gathered enough strength, attracts negative
people to me like a magnet. They, in turn, reinforce the put-downs
I tell myself. Sometimes I need to consciously put myself in situa-
tions with people who care about creativity as deeply as I do. Failing
that, hanging out with emotionally healthy people with positive at- ✗
titudes helps considerably.

We must do the work that these creative people are attempting
as they listen closely to their own thoughts, dispute the ones that
harm them, and insert thoughts that are better for them to hear. Like
Rosemary, we want to learn if our basic inner stance is self-punishing
and self-defeating. Like Jori, we want to get "on ourselves like glue"
when our thoughts are poised to send us on a downward spiral. Like
Kay, we need to recognize how negative thoughts lead to negative re- ✗
lationships.

Depression is caused in large measure by our negative feelings
about the facts of existence. We announce these feelings by our self-
talk. We have the chance to change our underlying feelings and avoid
depression by instantly disputing negative self-talk when it arises by
saying to the messenger, "This won't do! Go back and report that I
disagree!" By getting a grip on our mind, we actually change what we
think and what we feel.

OUR TANGLED MEANINGS AND MOTIVES

Our thoughts arise for real reasons and often for many reasons at
once, making them complex tangles of meanings. Even single words
like "best-seller," "composition," "talent," or "theory" are so loaded
with multiple meanings that each weighs a ton. A negative self-state-

ment like "I have no artistic talent" may stand for all of the following thoughts and feelings and many more:

+ "I am unwilling to try to draw because I know that my first drawings will embarrass me."

+ "Mixing colors must be very hard to learn. Probably I would just make mud."

+ "I don't really respect painting. Most modern art is silly, and classical art is outdated."

+ "It would be worse to be an amateur Sunday painter than to be no painter at all. How foolish I would look sitting out with my easel! How self-conscious I would feel!"

You might block a thought like "I have no artistic talent" and affirm that in fact you do have talent, but if you did so you would not really have learned what your negative self-statement meant. By eliminating it without examining it, root problems would likely remain. In addition to the three steps we have been discussing so far—thought identification, thought confrontation, and thought substitution—there is a fourth: understanding what we mean by what we say.

What does the innocent-sounding "I would love to write a novel" mean to someone who has dreamed of writing a novel but has never begun? Quite possibly it might mean, "I would really like to write a novel, but I have no ideas for a novel, no time to write a novel, no inclination to fail at writing a novel, and no hope of publishing the drivel I would probably write, so I won't try. But I prefer not to tell myself all that and confess my cowardice and my disinclination." If you get in the habit of suspecting that volumes of information and a tangle of motives lie hidden behind your self-statements, you will grow into heroic self-awareness.

Margaret Lucke, a writer and creativity coach, reflected on the idea of tangled meanings and tangled motives:

I recall a dinner-table conversation long ago when my father and my uncle were discussing the direction of their lives. Dad commented about how much he dreamed about doing such-and-such—I don't recall the specifics, but it was one of those "sail around the world" kind of things. Uncle Bill countered with, "Why don't you do it?" Dad listed all the responsibilities that kept him from pursuing his dream. "Then you don't want to sail around the world all that much," Uncle Bill replied. "What you want far more is to be what you consider a responsible person, and to have the comfort and respect that you gain from this nice home and your career and family. Ultimately, what people choose to do is what they really want to do, even if they claim to want something different."

A lively debate ensued about how and why people make certain choices. My uncle insisted that our choices express our true values or offer us some reward. Taking this action will help us further a goal, keep a promise, make a good impression, meet someone's expectations, advance our position in the community, fulfill a duty, enjoy a moment of pleasure, release anxiety, avoid an uncomfortable situation, or escape facing up to a fear. Many times these motives are obvious, but just as often, they can be hidden from our consciousness.

Since that conversation, when I'm confronted with a decision I have to make, I ask myself about each possible course of action: "What do I gain?" Sometimes the benefits are long-term and sometimes they are short-term. Sometimes they derive from my strengths, and at other times they are dictated by my weaknesses and fears. It has been tremendously helpful for me to take a long, hard look at what my true motives might be, to dig beneath the surface to try to discover what my subconscious wants as well as to articulate the desires that are fully apparent to me. Then comes the task of reconciling all these conflicting and competing desires.

We are fully capable of desiring many contradictory things, all at the same moment. Some of our hidden motives might seem to be unproductive or negative or even destructive, indicating an emotional or psychological resistance or block. Other motives might really be "shoulds"—things we don't really want to do but feel that we should do in order to be a good or successful person. But it is easily possible to want two or more things that would truly benefit our lives yet are difficult to make coexist—financial security and ample time to do our creative work, for example. The competition is often between what is pragmatic and feasible and the dream that seems more distant and difficult to attain.

Our tangle of meanings is often a tangle of motives. If a client says to me, "I want to get some new products together for an upcoming big crafts fair, but I would also love to do some painting," I might respond by saying, "Great. Both sound like worthwhile activities. I wonder if you might find it helpful to jot down some of the advantages of doing each. That might help to clarify your choices so that you could set your priorities effectively. What do you think?" This is not an interpretation, but rather an invitation for the client to interpret for herself what underlies her competing desires.

To interpret her statement directly, I might say, "I wonder if what you are considering here is finding a way to have the satisfaction of some immediate rewards. The crafts fair gives you the chance to show your work, enjoy the fellowship of other artists, and perhaps make a little money too. Painting can be lonely work and the payoff, other than your personal satisfaction in the process, could be far down the road where it's hard to see. Would you be more inclined to paint if we could find some ways to make your painting and your artistic self more visible in the world? What are your thoughts about this?"

Presenting one's work to the world and saying "I am an artist" requires great courage, which this artist may be unwilling or unready to muster for fear of the emotional consequences. So her response might be a denial of my interpretation and a refusal to look further at what is behind these competing desires. But perhaps her response would be positive, an acknowledgment that this interpretation has merit. At that point we might begin to think of ways to accomplish that goal of greater visibility, perhaps after the crafts fair is over. Another positive reaction could be a counterinterpretation on her part that demonstrates that although my take on her situation was wrong, thinking about it helped clarify her own perspective. In either case, the next step would be to figure out what to do to turn her new clarity into intentional action.

You are what you think. Meaning-making is impossible if your thoughts lead you about by the nose, if you have no way to dispute your negative thoughts, and if you can't penetrate to the real thoughts and feelings behind your customary expressions. Train yourself to hear what you are saying. Train yourself to confront your negative thoughts and to replace them with self-friendlier ones. Train yourself to look behind your words to discover what you actually mean. As with the other tasks I'm describing, this is a lot to ask. But asking anything less of yourself is a recipe for enduring depression.

5

OPTING TO MATTER

Brooding about meaning is depressing and unproductive. But stepping back, taking a deep breath, and examining meaning from the meta position, as an observer of your predicament and not the subject of a cruel joke, helps enormously. When you educate yourself about meaning, you begin to understand what freedom and responsibility entail. You realize that you must consciously decide to matter, that opting to matter is not a cosmic given but a necessary personal choice. As I am using the phrase, "opting to matter" means the following seven things:

1. Realizing and accepting that you have an ego, drives, desires, dreams, talents, a brain, a heart, and a complete human interior that makes potent demands on you. When overseen by ethics, this humanness should be heeded. You begin by accepting your human nature.

2. Announcing that you intend to process the information presented to you by life, come to your own conclusions about what life means and how you should act, and follow through on your conclusions. You are the sole arbiter of meaning.

3. Taking into account the "X" factor of your particular make-up and making as much sense as you can of your biology and your psychology. You are the only person who can understand you.

4. Living a righteous life, according to the ethical sense built right into you. You are your own moral compass.

5. Finding the energy to accomplish all of this, the way to activate your passion, enthusiasm, and life force. You are your own dynamo, your own generator of energy.

6. Taking charge of the present moment, the only moment available to you. You are the master of each moment.

7. Accepting and acknowledging that heroism will be required of you, if you decide to opt to matter. You must show courage.

Virtually no creative person reaches this high ideal. Most get mired in the first sense of opting to matter, the ego-driven sense, and consider that they are opting to matter if they create and achieve success in the marketplace. But the creative person whose only definition of opting to matter is to follow his desires will fail to meet his own ethical standards. He will experience repeated meaning crises since his pursuit of mere ego satisfactions will strike him as too limited a way to exist. Irritated that nothing satisfies him, driven to find the next exciting or ego-gratifying thing, he sets himself on the unhappy path of the petty tyrant.

The words that we associate with a person mattering in this limited egotistical sense are arrogance, selfishness, grandiosity, narcissism, and immaturity. Butterfield wrote of Bernini: "Bernini, high priest of Baroque sculpture, was as ruthless as any robber baron, stealing his colleagues' wives and ideas and highly susceptible to fits of violent rage." Freeman described Jung: "His personal life was a scandal, including affairs with other women in his home while his long-suffering wife was pregnant, purloining ideas from his disciples, and pursuing his personal interests with complete disregard of his family." Beaton wrote of Nureyev: "He was utterly self-centered, with no pity and no concern for others. He would say of people he knew, 'If they were dead, I wouldn't mind.' " Januszczak vividly described Caravaggio: "One of Europe's indisputably great painters, he was also a murderer, habitually violent, prone to bloody rages, always armed, always swaggering."

This is not what opting to matter means. Neither talent nor self-interest are excuses for ruthlessness. Too often the creative person presumes that his gift gives him the right to do whatever he pleases. Nicholas Berdyaev explained: "The greatness of creative genius is not correlative to moral perfection. A great artist may be an idle pleasure-seeker, 'one of the world's worthless children the most worthless he may be,' as Pushkin put it. Creative genius is bestowed on man for nothing and is not connected with his moral or religious efforts to attain perfection." You may be born creative, but you must *decide* to be good. A complete definition of opting to matter includes an injunction against lording it over others simply because you feel unique and special.

FUELING THE DECISION TO MATTER

How influential was it on the young van Gogh to be forced to visit the gravesite of his deceased younger brother and namesake, the first Vincent van Gogh? How influential was it to be born into a pious, bourgeois, mercantile culture, one in which profits and a vengeful God were strictly worshipped? How influential was it to grow up under perpetually gray skies? How influential was it to decide to live on the largess of his brother Theo? How influential was it to walk away from the boy who might or might not have been his son? No one knows, Vincent van Gogh included.

We don't know the secret of our own genetics, how easy or hard it is for us to change our basic nature, or how our beliefs are woven together. This "X" factor produces, if not utter mystery, enough mystery that our understanding of who we are is obscured and limited. But if we are to opt to matter, we must make the effort, however futile, to solve the mystery of ourselves. What if you learn, as van Gogh would have learned, that your chilly upbringing has made you exceptionally vulnerable to meaning crises? Your way to meaning will then require a great deal more than traveling to the south of France for the sun and the bright colors. You will need to transform and heal yourself, for only transformation and healing will make you a person who can manage meaning effectively.

Until you come to grips with your personality and your human nature and can say, "This is who I am and this is who I am choosing to become," not only will meaning elude you but so will a genuine enthusiasm for life. Without this transformation, you may appear energetic, like the van Gogh who painted 200 paintings in a year, but in fact you will have succumbed to a mania that must, as it runs its course, end in depression. Without a genuine passion for life, which only comes with self-understanding, your decision to matter will remain a strictly intellectual one.

Once you gain self-understanding, you will still have to throw the switch and demand that your energy return. Passion will only flow if it has your permission to flow. Think of your life right now. Are you energetic in your life pursuits, full of fire as you approach your writing or your research, full of curiosity and enthusiasm, a live wire? Few creative individuals are like this. Most are slowed down by the

facts of existence, more tired than passionate, more indifferent than curious. Over time, they have shut down their own power supply.

But the energy is not gone. The simplest proof is that a person can lift a car to rescue her child and march thousands of miles to protect her country. That potential energy remains locked within us, unavailable most of the time because we doubt that anything much will come of unleashing it. Rev up to write another article? Ho-hum. Go on all cylinders to get to my day job? Yawn. Write another screenplay that no one wants? Boring! It is as if we had a nuclear reactor within us but saw nothing on the horizon but a light bulb to light. Who would be motivated to put a nuclear plant on-line for such a paltry reward?

Yet the answer is to bring that plant on-line. You must throw the switch on your desire and let it flood back. You may find this a brilliant idea, to simply throw the switch and let your passion flood back, but in your secret heart you are likely to feel frightened. You may doubt that you'd make good use of all that energy. You may anticipate disappointment, reckoning that the passion you ignite will just go to waste on some project that you might bungle. You may feel scared about flooding yourself with all that kilowatt power and turning yourself into a wild man or woman. In short, you may not want to do this thing—throw the switch—even though you understand that it's exactly what you must do. Are you willing to turn yourself into a fiery person, someone who burns hotter than her neighbors?

If you want to opt to matter, you must throw the switch. You have the key to unlock the fuel box. Of course, you may face the most tangled complications, from a chronic illness to an anxiety disorder, from relentless life fatigue to a phlegmatic personality. You may have a hundred reasons not to release your energy and a score of obstacles between you and the chance to burn brightly. As with every other task that I'm describing, all you can do is make a sincere effort in the desired direction. Whatever reasons you have for not throwing the switch and whatever obstacles stand between you and your energy, try to light your fire.

THE MODERN HISTORY OF NOT MATTERING

It would seem self-evident that a person would opt to matter. Why wouldn't he? Certainly, his upbringing might be one impediment. He might have grown up lectured about the extent to which he didn't matter and punished for attempting to matter. His culture, too, might have drilled into him the idea that he was merely one of many and that group norms always came first: that religion came first, fitting in came first, not making waves came first. Many life lessons might have taught him that it was wrong or pointless to opt to matter.

Still, the magnitude of his difficulty in opting to matter is not really explained even by these many negative life lessons. It turns out that the main obstacle he faces is his belief, shared by every modern person, that human life is meaningless. Any reasons that he tries to adduce for mattering are overwhelmed by the possibility, bordering on a certainty, that he and his fellow human beings are only excited matter, put on earth for no reason except that the universe could do it. All life, his included, is mere pointless happenstance, not worth crying about or taking seriously.

This bitter pill is a new view, barely 200 years old. Before that, life seemed special. For thousands of years, the idea of life as categorically different from nonlife, unique and important in the cosmos, was a core tenet of natural philosophy. A typical argument from the old school is that of 19th-century biologist Schubert-Soldern:

> Inorganic chemical compounds do not give rise to organic ones. If the forces at work in inorganic nature are always bound up with atoms and molecules, and if these of themselves can never produce organic compounds, it must follow that the inorganic forces by themselves are incapable of forming anything organic. From this we may conclude that the organic compounds arise not simply from the elements, but only through the operation of life; the inorganic forces are insufficient of themselves to build up organic compounds.

This argument, a tenet of the philosophy known as vitalism, seemed compelling until biologists found, beginning with Wöhler and the synthesis of urea in 1828, that organic compounds could indeed be created from inorganic materials. We can date our present difficulties in making and maintaining meaning from that single event, the synthesis of urea. From that day forward, a new philosophy was needed since life lost much of its mystery, sanctity, importance, and glamour.

Once you join the scientific materialists, as all of us have to a lesser or a greater degree, and believe that you can make human beings simply by striking dead atoms with powerful but meaningless forces, life turns meaningless. This is the basic problem with which we've been wrestling for 200 years. To be sure, religions and spiritual beliefs are more popular than ever, and ancient vitalist arguments are still upheld in every church. But the suspicion that we do not matter haunts and plagues those of us who are existential; that is, everyone who creates.

We manage to bear up despite the suspicion that we are merely excited matter. We find ways to bear up every day. But on many days we discover that we can't bear up; on those days we despair about our cosmic unimportance and grow furious with the facts of existence. We feel saddened and defeated and lose our motivation to create or to make meaning in any way. The very word "meaning" strikes our ears as a cosmic joke. Because of our fear that we are merely excited matter and the consequent grudge that we hold against the universe, we feel lost and alienated, like a refugee far from home in a universe that cares nothing for us.

Every creative person, believer or nonbeliever, is modern and postmodern enough to doubt whether the word "meaning" really signifies anything. If, by chance, it does, it is still an open question whether it signifies anything worth caring about. We fear that the word "meaningful" is a chimera, a high-sounding word that signifies little more than "what I like" or "what I believe." Are our questions about meaning mere questions about likes and dislikes, on the order of "Do I prefer strawberry ice cream to vanilla ice cream?" We suspect that they are.

Battered by these thoughts, a creator is driven to throw up her hands and cry, "Why bother! Why wrestle this stupid novel into existence? I might as well find some simple pleasures, eat chocolate, take a bubble bath, and to hell with the idea of making meaning!" So she eats chocolate and takes a bubble bath. But within minutes she is forcibly struck by a counterthought. A countervailing energy rises in her, something like hope and something like pride, which readies her to do combat with her sincere belief that she is utterly unimportant.

COMING BACK TO MATTERING

When creative people try to throw up their hands and resign themselves to accepting postmodern meaninglessness and the illusory nature of meaning, they find that they can't. "Meaning" continues to vibrate in a way that convinces them that, while it may be a difficult and even a suspect word, it is not an empty word. Meaning means something and, therefore, an authentic life is possible. At the last instant, ready to embrace the terrible fruits of deconstruction, creative people return with a vengeance to the belief that a meaningful life can be led and that they are obliged to choose that way.

In our hearts, we opt for life. We opt to live the 20 years or the 60 years ahead of us. This may be all that we have, but it is exactly what we have. As Schubert-Soldern aphoristically put it, "To understand life, we must contrast it with death." We force life to mean because we are alive and not dead. We force life to mean while we are alive and until death releases us from our responsibility to live authentically. We say, "While I am alive, I can love." We say, "While I am alive, I can learn a few things." We say, "While I am alive, I can help in some ways." We say, "While I am alive, I can create." We live because we can and because, unromantically but utterly sincerely, we must.

In the two decades after the Second World War, when the French existentialists Camus and Sartre were becoming worldwide figures and the philosophy dubbed existentialism was gaining millions of interested readers, it looked like issues of personal freedom and meaning-making might become subjects of deep, abiding interest to creative individuals everywhere. But people retreated from the demands that existentialism posited. Even creative people found it impossible to look life squarely in the eye and announce, "I am the final, complete arbiter of meaning. The only meaning my life can have is the meaning with which I invest it." The dark void pointed to by the existentialists was really a kind of Zen stripping down to the essential choices of life—to be ethical, to accept personal responsibility, to really live—and the demanding nature of these choices scared most people off.

The most important shift for the contemporary creator to make is the one demanded by the existentialists, the shift from the despairing "Why do I exist?" to the steely "I exist." A creator must stop pestering himself with the unanswerable questions that plague him— the need to know why he is alive, who or what made the universe, who can tell him about the meaning of life, what are the first or final causes—and accept as his mantra, "I am alive."

In his aliveness he finds everything he needs to know about how to live. All he needs to do is accept his purest understanding of his own meaning-making responsibilities. He doesn't have to adapt to existence any more than a bird has to adapt to the sky. He and existence are already adapted together. He simply has to accept that he is the only possible maker of personal meaning. Part of him wants to cry out, "I don't belong here, there's no place for me here, the hell with it!" But he does belong here, and he must pull his chair up to the table.

Even if he manages to do this, the postmodern coloration will persist. In a corner of his mind, a creator is always this close to believing that meaning is an illusion and that meaninglessness is the true state of affairs. The best he can do is inoculate himself against this potential loss of meaning, and consequent depression, by devoting another corner of his mind to the rejoinder that meaning is not an illusion and that his life can be made to mean. This is the dynamic tension that adds unwanted stress to every contemporary creator's life but that really can't be avoided: Poised on the brink of meaninglessness, a creator must repeatedly fight his way back to meaning.

You take the postmodern coloration into account by refusing to entertain the idea that meaning is a meaningless word. Meaning may well not mean what we would like it to mean. It may only mean something like "that which my human nature elevates to a high status, even though that elevation is of no concern to the universe at large." Even if it means just that, then meaning has meaning for you. It may be a folly and a gamble to make this deal with yourself—to announce that "meaning means" and that it must mean until you cease to exist—but it is the right folly and the only good game in town.

We opt to matter irrespective of the fact that life stands squarely in the way of our ability to matter. If we refuse to opt to matter, our meaning-making efforts peter out, and we end up settling for second-rate meaning substitutes or meaninglessness, each with its attendant depression. But if we hold ourselves up to a lofty, entirely self-imposed standard—that we are determined to matter, in accordance with our highest principles—then we imbue our meaning-making efforts with the seriousness that we know they require.

Opting to matter does not answer every meaning question, nor is it a complete depression treatment program in and of itself. It alone will not make a boring meeting meaningful or a mistake that ruins a novel a pleasant experience. It alone will not keep meaning afloat on gloomy days when nothing feels worth attempting. It alone will not cure a hormonal imbalance or end an arctic winter. Still, it is a vital step on the path to meaningful living. Once meaning becomes an issue, as it does for every creator, a state of crisis exists, and crisis management begins with the decision to matter.

In his book *The Pursuit of Meaning*, Joseph Fabry explained:

> An art professor at Sacramento State College observed that students often panic when confronting an empty canvas and are unable to paint. They experience the existential vacuum of the contemporary painter: no style is required, no tasks are demanded of them. After the shock of the empty canvas subsides, the students often go back to old masterpieces to search for significance or to slavishly copy the past. Students panicking before the empty canvas are the prototype of many people today, free to do as they please.

A painter facing a blank canvas, a writer facing a blank computer screen, an actor facing a cattle call audition, a researcher facing a mass of data all face this postmodern question: "Do I or my efforts matter?" As Irvin Yalom put it, "How does a being who needs meaning find meaning in a universe that has no meaning?" At first glance, there seems to be no answer to this terrible question. But the answer is straightforward. We have been given life. Part of our inheritance is human consciousness. Out of this very human consciousness arises the idea that we can live righteously and meaningfully. Therefore, we can opt to do just that. Maybe we are trivial creatures in a trivial universe. Will you allow that suspicion—even that fact— to paralyze you?

6

RECKONING WITH THE FACTS OF EXISTENCE

Opting to matter means affirming your rights and responsibilities as a conscious, righteous human being. You announce that you have it in you to live an eloquent, productive, ethical life, your personal and human shortcomings notwithstanding. You commit to turning your meaningful life plan into reality. After you have reflected on meaning and walked yourself through a thorough existential examination of your situation, you conclude that you will operate as if you matter, irrespective of the potent reasons arrayed against such a conclusion. If you only do this work in front of a mirror and fail to take the realities of the world into account, however, you are doing little more than wishing, dreaming, and fantasizing.

You must reckon with the facts of existence so as to know what you must do in order to lead a righteous, creative life. Is your own personality a problem? You look that fact of existence squarely in the eye. Is the creative discipline you have chosen as your prime meaning container one that can't earn you a living? You look that fact of existence squarely in the eye. Of course you blink because you are human, but you return your gaze to reality as soon as you are able because the answers you need can only be found in the real world.

What are these "facts of existence" with which a creative person must reckon? At a minimum, they include the shape of each creative discipline, the nature of the creative process, and the nature of the species. Jack Kerouac, that Dharma bum, relentlessly networked because he reckoned that networking was a fact of life for any writer who wanted an audience. One writer will reckon with this fact while most will not. A physicist might find himself more in agreement with a rival theory than with his own but refuse to switch sides because of stubborn pride. Because of his ego and his need to protect his standing, his refusal to reckon with the facts pertinent to his existence will cost him years of depression.

You do this reckoning by being honest and courageous. What do you need to do in order to write 20 worthy books over the next 30 years? You must write. You must find a way to survive, one that doesn't kill your soul or drain every ounce of energy from your body. You must go into the unknown where the writing lives. You must transcend your weaknesses of character. You must turn a clear-eyed gaze on the publishing marketplace. If your narrative requires an excellent plot twist at the end, then you must plot that twist. None of this is secret information available to only a select few. You already know this, but you must reckon with it honestly and courageously.

A devastating war may erupt. The French existentialists who lived through World War II wrote eloquently about how those terrible facts of existence tested everyone. Each creator had new, unavoidable reckoning to do. As a result, some joined the Resistance, as Camus did; some comforted the populace while talking back to tyrants, as Shostakovich did; some marched proudly into the gas ovens—Jew,

Gypsy, and German alike—never repudiating their opposition to the Third Reich. Is an Israeli painter or a Palestinian filmmaker any less tested today? An Anglican biologist in Dublin or a Catholic geologist in Belfast? Or anyone anywhere? This reckoning never ends.

Creators know that they must reckon with all of this, but they don't feel equal to the task. No one is equal to the task. Everyone is in the same boat—an Einstein and a shoemaker, a Harvard professor and his heroin-addicted brother, a television celebrity and her girl-friends from the neighborhood—unequal to the demands that reality makes. The customary way to handle this insufficiency is to turn a blind eye to the facts of existence and to deal with only a tiny portion allowed to pass in through one half-shut eye. But we must do better.

You reckon with the facts of existence by asking yourself pertinent questions, noting where you slipped in the past, acknowledging the shadows in your personality, and determining which principles you in-tend to embody. The Chinese philosopher Fung Yu-Lan posited four spheres of living: the innocent and the utilitarian spheres, where man is merely as he is; and the moral and the transcendent spheres, where man is as he ought to be. The authentic creator reckons with the facts of existence not to provide himself with utilitarian answers to practical questions like how to get published or how to acquire tenure, but so as to operate in the moral sphere and the transcendent sphere. In this latter place, as Fung envisioned it, we exist "with a knowledge of Heaven, in service of Heaven, in unity with Heaven, and enjoying Heaven." Heaven or no heaven, we do this just to live authentically.

DREAMING LARGE WHILE REALITY-TESTING

In his essay "Create Dangerously," Albert Camus wrote, "The loftiest work will always be, as in the Greek tragedians, Melville, Tolstoy, or

Molière, the work that maintains an equilibrium between reality and man's rejection of that reality, each forcing the other upward in a ceaseless overflowing, characteristic of life itself at its most joyous and heart-rending extremes." Creators must do this same tense balancing work: They must dream large and affirm what is best for the species, but they must also reckon with the facts of existence exactly as they find them.

When I train creativity coaches, I advise them that creators are obliged to dream large and opt to matter, but they are also obliged to reality-test and reckon with the facts of existence. The following are three responses from coaches to this suggestion.

David Stringham, a psychologist and creativity coach, observed:

> The issue of dream-upholding and reality-testing is prominent for me with one of my clients. This person is a songwriter, trying to market his songs to the music industry. As we were establishing what to focus on in coaching, he felt he needed more help with creative marketing rather than songwriting, so that has been our focus. He currently has a job as a professional in another field but wants his music business to get to the point that he can support himself with the music and quit his other job. He has expressed a lot of frustration with his inability to do this. For me, the main aspect of reality-testing versus dream-upholding is in his desire, actually an expectation on himself, to have music be his only source of income. As long as he is dependent on his other job, he feels like a failure.
>
> I was a musician for many years, and I knew many very talented and gifted musicians who were playing and performing regularly but still needed other means of income. On the one hand, I don't want to blindly support his dream and build up false hopes, which will cause him to devalue the work that he is doing because he isn't making a living doing it. On the other hand, I don't want

to paint an unrealistically bleak picture based on my own experience. There are people who are making a good living writing sound tracks for soap operas, TV commercials, etc. Could he join their ranks?

Through him, I may even be vicariously pursuing a path that I didn't take. Working with him in this area is arousing some demons of my own. In my own history, I was a professional musician for 15 years. I had many dreams, some fulfilled, some not. I fulfilled my dreams of playing in bands regularly, playing music that I loved, developing my improvisational skills, and soloing often. I composed music and made sound tracks for modern dances and fulfilled dreams of hearing my music performed in wonderful settings. I fulfilled my dream of supporting myself as a musician, although it was very modest (on the verge of poverty at times). I didn't fulfill other dreams such as being a big star, becoming a commercial success, or becoming a commercially successful songwriter.

As far as the songwriting went, I did write quite a bit of music but never took the next step to market it. At the time, marketing seemed mysterious to me. I beat myself up for not being able to market my songs. I felt that I should have been able to do this but still I was unable to. I knew I was stuck—I suspected I was blocked—but I couldn't get unstuck. Now, in retrospect, I see I was blocked in the last stage of the creative process, the stage of "showing your work." I could take all sorts of risks on stage in front of hundreds of people, showing my work, but I was unable to pick up a phone to make cold calls to people in the industry to try to sell my songs. Subconsciously, I avoided the anxiety of presenting my songs to people in the industry by never seeming to find the time to do it or being unable to figure out how to do it.

As I deal with my client marketing himself in the music industry, I am reminded about how blocked I was in this area. I am *using this as an opportunity to see if these same blocks are pre-senting themselves in my current profession. Am I spending a lot of time researching and preparing to be a coach but still blocking in that crucial area of truly selling myself? Are the same dynamics that prevented me from selling myself to record companies interfering with my efforts to sell myself as a creativity coach? I've got my own work to do.*

Kay Porterfield, a writer and creativity coach, described the movement made by one of her clients from defensiveness to awareness:

Over the long haul, we can work toward finding a balance be-tween our dreams and reality. One of my clients has been swinging on this pendulum since we began this coaching process. She wrote some folktales, then reality-tested and decided she wasn't willing to make the time investment of working on them further and then mar-keting them. She wanted income, and she wanted it now. I asked her what she could do to make immediate money and, at the same time, perhaps further her long-term goal. She decided that book reviews might be a partial answer, and she began working on some book re-views for a local newspaper. But she got totally stuck on one book—paralyzed, I would say—and didn't contact me for about three weeks.

Today she called to say that the book, a novel, had brought up profound issues for her about boarding school, her parents, and the life-long defenses she developed because of those experiences. "I've been living a lie," she said and explained that she had been reacting all of her life to these early experiences and at the same time vehe-mently denying that they had affected her. She said she was disap-pointed and angry at the book she'd read for what the author hadn't said. I listened as she talked about some of her experiences and how she felt about them. Suddenly she stopped short and said that she knew what she had to do—go to the country, set up a workspace in a relative's spare bedroom, and start writing her truth about private schools.

I could feel the shift in energy over the phone. At one point in my life, I would have been impatient with her earlier flip-flopping, and I would have been more concerned with trying to get her to focus. Today I believe that that foundering is part of the process and that we've got to trust the process, encouraging our clients at the same time that we serve as their safety net. Who knows when this move toward authenticity would have come if she hadn't "sidetracked" and read that novel, thinking that she'd make some fast cash? Of course, this is a face of the absurdity that existentialists talk about. In my own life, absurdity used to stymie more than it does now. Now, I see it as a trickster bearing gifts.

Ellen Silverstein, a songwriter and creativity coach, observed:

Ah, the dream versus reality—that is really the crux of the matter not only for our clients but for ourselves, as coaches and as creative individuals striving to do our own meaningful work. Gandhi said, "Whatever you do will be insignificant, but it is very important that you do it." I try to remember this crucial idea whenever I'm beset by the "Why bother?" blues, when I hear that whiny song in my head that says, "Who cares? What's the point of trying? The last thing the world needs is yet another unnoticed book/song/poem/painting. What difference does it make?"

Well, it makes a huge difference to me. The whole of my life goes more smoothly when I am making consistent progress on a creative project. I was struck by the lesson's definition of an authentic life: one in which we "honor and assimilate truths about the human condition and plot a righteous and reasoned course that is rich in dreams and rich in action." An excellent goal, I think. I am good at the dreams but I have a lot of work to do when it comes to the action.

Any effort that a lone individual makes may not change the

world, but the cumulative effect of small individual efforts can be enormous. And we can never know what our work might bring about. To take one example, I was deeply touched and gratified to receive a letter from a stranger who had read a story I had written. He was inspired by it to contact his long-estranged son and begin to work toward a reconciliation. It is difficult to continue to believe in yourself and the importance of your work when the world seems so indifferent. In the American culture, success is defined almost solely in monetary terms—we are defined by what we do for a living, and our success is measured by how sumptuous a living we earn. It is an easy jump to assume that if we cannot manage to earn a living through our creative work, then we are failures and our work must be worthless. How sad this is, and how short-sighted.

It is easy to conclude that we must abandon our creative project in favor of whatever activity puts the roof over our head and the bread on our table. One of my clients recently wrote to me, "I need to deal with the issue of money—it's always where I go with my fear and always the issue that saps my creative energy." I easily could have written those words myself, for I grapple constantly with the same issue.

No one can list all of the facts of existence that confront us. The toothache of Dostoyevsky's Underground Man, the sudden Franco-Prussian war that engulfed the Impressionists, a new technology that renders your lifelong craft obsolete—the list rumbles on like an endless freight train passing in the night. The facts of existence can't be counted or halted. But those are not our tasks. Our tasks are to reckon with them and to refuse to let them defeat us.

THE ELOQUENT TRUTH

There are ordinary truths and eloquent truths. The ordinary truth is that some painters can garner six figures for their canvases while you probably can't. The eloquent truth is that this abrasive fact need not alter your resolve to live an authentic life. The ordinary truth is that you will make mistakes and messes and fall short many times. The eloquent truth is that this need not defeat you, that you can keep trying and that you can keep kicking. When you marry these two ideas—willing yourself to matter and willing yourself to reckon with the facts of existence—your truth becomes more eloquent.

Dru Simms, a writer and creativity coach, explained:

> An authentic life means that I must be committed to seeking what is true for me and how to live congruently with that truth. Since life does not lend itself to simple solutions, the challenge of addressing personal authenticity is not simple or easy. It requires a kind of existential courage, which there is no guarantee I can find or maintain. In every moment, whether I am conscious of it or not, I make a choice either away from or toward my authentic self.
>
> While the conscious search for personal truth has been a life-long motivation for me, it has become an urgent priority in recent years. Life crises, and perhaps just the force of having gained "a certain age," have inspired me to a greater focus on these issues. A few years ago, I kept hearing myself wail, "What about ME?" This sounded terribly self-pitying, and I was embarrassed to be saying it, but as I listened more closely, I recognized it as a call to ask deeper questions: "How can I get myself to stand up for myself?" "How do I represent my authentic self to others?" and "Who am I really—what is it that I want to stand up for in the first place?"
>
> Direct statements about wanting to live an authentic life now show up often across my life—in my thoughts, in my writing, in the way I stand before creative projects, and in discussions with others, especially with friends who are also interested in this quest for themselves. These statements remind me that I am seeking to be present with my own inner truth through whatever happens.
>
> My commitment to an authentic life is a challenge and a gift.

It is a spiritual practice, a practical art, a relational skill, and an imperfect quest, which I know will never be complete. I experience this quest as gripping, exhilarating, awe-inspiring, and a genesis for creativity and deeper relationships. I also experience it as frightening, tedious, exhausting, and dangerous. I know that it is not necessary, or even possible, to accomplish this quest in any perfect way. But to remind myself of its elusive nature, I carry around a quote from Anaïs Nin: "The dream is always running ahead. To catch up, to live for a moment in unison with it, that is the miracle."

All of these things I try to remember when working with my clients. I try to remember that each person's perception of what is meant by an authentic life is by definition unique and that they are walking the same tightrope between their false life and their true life as I am. I try to remember that only they can define their personal truths, and only they can choose to explore those truths through their work or anywhere else in their lives. I also try to remember that simple encouragement from another kindred spirit really can help and that, as nearly as I can tell, seeking to live authentically is far better than any alternative.

You should be reminded of Sisyphus, who was doomed to toil for all time rolling a stone up a mountain but who rebelled by asserting an essential freedom of attitude. The myth of Sisyphus and his stone is the story of a man reckoning with the facts of existence and not succumbing to them. Had he succumbed to them, he would have been left with nothing but an eternity of pain. Here is how the Camus essay "The Myth of Sisyphus" ends: "Sisyphus teaches the higher fidelity that negates the gods and raises rocks. He concludes that all is well. This universe henceforth without a master seems to him neither sterile nor futile. Each atom of that stone, each mineral flake of that night-filled mountain, in itself forms a world. The struggle toward the heights is enough to fill a man's heart. One must imagine Sisyphus happy."

A creator's task is to reckon with the facts of existence very much as Sisyphus reckons with his situation. Viewed one way, Sisyphus is a victim of a cruel, harsh, punitive universe. Any creator might come to the same conclusion about his situation, were he to tote up the facts of existence not to his liking. But Sisyphus has decided to force his life to mean. He makes use of the freedom at his disposal and reckons that, as he is not dead, he still has meaning to make. It may be the height of absurdity to call Sisyphus happy. But if that is his defiant claim, who can argue with him?

7

BRAVING ANXIETY

When we perceive a threat, we get queasy, light headed, confused, agitated, fatigued, nervous. We call these various reactions to a perceived threat by one name: anxiety. Existence threatens us in a thousand ways and therefore, anxiety is our constant companion. If we reacted less dramatically to perceived threats, we might have the chance to handle them more efficiently. But Nature has decided to err on the side of caution. She has endowed us with large reactions to small dangers. Writing a short story, say, is really only a small threat to our self-esteem since if we do a poor job, we can revise our story or write a better one. But nature has decided that even these tiny threats must be taken very seriously. As soon as we say, "I want to write a short story," waves of anxiety arise to keep us out of harm's way.

The net result is that we do not write the story and do not make any meaning. Since we are not making meaning, depression strikes. The relationship between anxiety and depression, therefore, is direct and significant. If existence merely troubled us but didn't rouse so much anxiety in us, if we could hold our painting or composing as hard but not threatening, we would have a far better chance of making meaning and avoiding depression. If we heard ourselves say, "I don't want to paint because I don't find painting meaningful," we could reply instantly, "The heck with you, insidious thought! I'm off to the studio!" But because the thought is threatening and because Nature hates threats, we are bathed in anxiety and stopped in our tracks.

Since we experience a thought like "painting is not meaningful" as dangerous, as a threat to our identity and to our life plan, we respond to it with a whole array of biological and psychological defenses meant to ward off danger. If the threat were external, we would fight or flee. With internal threats, we generally flee from them rather than fight them. Our primary defense is to muffle the thought, not really hear it, and drown it out under a tidal wave of hormones and defensive counterthoughts. As a result, we have little idea what really just transpired.

We had a fleeting thought that we can no longer identify, we reacted with anxiety and defensiveness, the moment passed, and all we know for sure is that we are not going to the studio. This painful cycle—threatening thought, anxious reaction, and full retreat—is a fundamental cycle in the lives of creative people. Most creators are not aware of the existence of this cycle or that anxiety is a mighty brake preventing them from creating and from making meaning. Most creators do not give anxiety its due.

If you don't write your nonfiction book, which you have every reason to write and which you have been talking about writing for years, it is unlikely that you will call your blockage a phobia and point to anxiety as the culprit. If, in the middle of practicing your musical instrument, you experience terrible pains which, when you visit the doctor, can't be explained medically, you will probably go to the next doctor (or chiropractor, acupuncturist, or herbalist) rather than name anxiety as the culprit. If you obsess about a single color and paint monochromatically for a decade while harboring the suspicion that many important painting encounters are eluding you, it is doubtful that you will ask yourself, "What part is anxiety playing in my obsession?"

Anxiety is causing all of this: the indecisiveness, the mental fog, the physical pain, the loss of energy, the creative blockage, deflections and displacements of all sorts. One client, a well-known writer, spent virtually every morning thinking about his stockbroker. He didn't trust him and wanted to fire him. But the stockbroker was a close friend of his father, whom he didn't want to upset. There were plenty of rational ways to approach this impasse, if the impasse had been about the stockbroker. But it wasn't. This writer's internal debate about his stockbroker was the way his anxiety about writing played itself out.

Another client, a painter, claimed that the reason she wasn't painting was because she intensely disliked the watercolor paper she was using. There was only one brand she really liked, but that brand was very hard to find. Her half-hearted attempts at locating a large quantity of that special paper so far had failed. Of course, there were plenty of ways to get that paper, if the matter had really been about acquiring the right paper. A few well-placed phone calls would have ended the problem. But not having the right paper wasn't the issue. The issue was the anxiety that thinking about painting provoked in her.

Many of the clients I see complain of procrastination. Instead of starting off a Sunday turning right to their creative efforts, first they write in their journal, then they read the newspaper, then they have a third cup of coffee, then they head out to the Laundromat. It turns out that they will do almost anything to ward off the anxiety they might feel if they said to themselves, "Time to create!" While at work, they tell themselves that they will get to their novel or their symphony as soon as they get home, or after dinner at the latest. When they get home, they look at the ads that came in that day's mail, make dinner, do the dishes, and watch television until bedtime. Anxiety steals away their evening.

When a creator does this frequently enough and lets his anxiety about creating stop him from creating, he begins to feel like a weak, indecisive person. It is a very short step to even darker feelings of worthlessness and hopelessness. The end result of not knowing that he must brave his anxiety is that he ends up completely down on himself. Anxiety bests him and, to make matters worse, he then has to deal with the negative labels he pins on himself. This classic vicious cycle, where anxiety leads to a battered self-image and a battered self-image makes it harder to brave anxiety, defeats many creators.

Anxiety can debilitate any creator, even the most strong-willed and self-directing. A fiercely independent-minded sculptor may mention with a laugh that some friends visited his studio and hated his new work. On the surface, it looks like he's shrugged their comments off. Three weeks later, he complains of serious blockage. Doubts about his talent now make him anxious, his anxiety causes him not to sculpt, but the "why" of this is completely unknown to him. Anxiety has chalked up another victim.

PRIMARY EXISTENTIAL ANXIETY

Anxiety can arise from any threat, from the threat of earthquakes or nuclear weapons to the threat of snakes or public speaking. But the gravest threat that creators face, and hence the source of the most profound anxiety, are threats to meaning. Primary existential anxiety wells up in us when we try to make meaning, when we are thwarted in our efforts to make meaning, and when we are confronted by meaning drains, meaning losses, and other meaning problems. This is the anxiety we experience when we doubt our motives, our beliefs, and other core elements of our existence.

When we discuss our literary projects with editors and literary agents, this is the anxiety we experience since much of our personal meaning is at stake at such times. When we learn that our scientific theory may be flawed, this is the anxiety we experience since much of our meaning is invested in our theory. When we doubt that we know what life means or what our life is supposed to mean, when a threat arises that puts our belief system or our life plan in danger, primary existential anxiety wells up, rendering us that much less able to maintain meaning.

Consider the following experiment from social psychology. A pair of researchers, Birney and Houston, studied to what extent a subject's aesthetic preferences would be affected by peer pressure. A subject was asked to select his favorite paintings from among an array of paintings. Then, a few weeks later, he was asked to rerate his preferences, this time in the company of other "subjects" who were confederates of the experimenter. The confederates expressed their preferences first, before the subject rerated his. Sometimes the choices confederates selected were very similar to the subject's, and sometimes they were quite contrary.

After the confederates "rerated their preferences," the subject rerated his. When confronted by antagonistic views, all subjects yielded, changing their minds at least a little about which paintings they preferred. Birney and Houston reported that "subjects high in creativity, as measured by Barron's devices, yielded least, but all subjects showed considerable yielding even though personal esthetic preferences were involved."

Were the subjects yielding to peer pressure? Possibly. But more likely the contrary reports of their peers made them doubt not just their preferences, but their very ability to judge. It is easy enough to enjoy an all-blue painting, a political caricature, an old master, a Picasso, a surrealist collage, or anything under the sun, just as long as you don't have to ask yourself the question, "Do I find this painting really meaningful?" As soon as that question enters the picture, as it must have for these subjects, existential doubt rears its ugly head, followed immediately by existential anxiety.

A person who does not question meaning or need to force life to mean does not have to defend himself against thoughts that might provoke a meaning crisis. He is therefore blissfully that much less anxious than someone who is struggling to maintain meaning. It might be taken as a further bit of cosmic irony that people who have the most to offer—composers, writers, painters, scientists—must make their offerings while burdened by anxiety. But they must. Creative people are anxious not because they are neurotic but because the meaning crises they experience precipitate anxiety.

Because of the plentiful anxiety symptoms we see in creative people, it has been customary to adduce biological or psychological reasons for the presence of this anxiety. Maybe creative people are the biologically anxious offspring of biologically anxious parents. Maybe anxiety runs in their families. Maybe they are psychologically "highly sensitive" and prone to anxiety because they are inundated by sense data. But it is more likely that the anxiety we see is the result of the heroic effort the creative person is making trying to force life to mean. His brave efforts make him feel threatened at every turn, whenever he thinks about going into the unknown to create and whenever he tries to wrestle a new creation into existence.

CONFLICTUAL ANXIETY

In addition to the primary existential anxiety that afflicts creative people, there is anxiety arising from many other sources. The second most potent anxiety-producer is inner conflict. A person who is holding two opposing beliefs, one overt and one covert, is bound to react to this "unconscious" conflict with anxiety. These conflicts involve an "acceptable" belief, which the creator takes as his real and only motivation, and an "unacceptable" belief, which the creator endeavors to keep himself from knowing.

The conflict might be between the overt belief, "I am a musician," and the covert belief, "My parents made me become a musician. I never wanted this life!" This conflict can produce a hard-working but tortured musician prone to severe bouts of performance anxiety. The conflict might be between the overt belief, "People are good, and I'm a nice person," and the covert belief, "People have been mean to me, and I will get my revenge!" This conflict produces a passive-aggressive personality. The conflict might be between the overt belief, "I have a lot to say about the work I do," and the covert belief, "I have nothing new or important to contribute." This conflict produces a blocked psychiatrist, anthropologist, or economist who never gets his articles or books written.

Rollo May, distinguishing conflictual anxiety from existential anxiety, characterized conflictual anxiety in the following way:

> Suppose a young man, a musician, goes out on his first date, and for reasons he cannot understand he is very much afraid of the girl and has a fairly miserable time. Then suppose he dodges this real problem by vowing to cut girls out of his life and devote himself to his music. However, a few years later, as a successful bachelor musician, he finds he is very strangely inhibited around women, cannot speak to them without blushing, is afraid of his secretary, and scared to death of the women chairmen of committees with whom he must deal in arranging his concert schedule. He can find no objective reason for being so frightened, for he knows the women in actual fact hold very little power over him. He is experiencing neurotic anxiety—that is, anxiety disproportionate to the real danger and arising from an unconscious conflict within himself.

A creator burdened by the added vulnerabilities that arise from childhood experiences of criticism, rejection, abuse, abandonment, brainwashing, or similar structure-altering trauma is particularly likely to harbor inner conflicts. As a result, he will organize his personality around warding off his covert thoughts and fanatically following his overt thoughts. Such a person is on the run from himself, in flight from the experience of anxiety and fueled by the dynamic energy of conflict. Added vulnerabilities or not, however, we are all vulnerable to the terrors of conflictual anxiety. If we claim to matter but don't really believe it, if we hope that our creative work will touch other people but doubt that it will, if we argue that the gamble we took becoming an actor or a dancer was worth it but secretly wonder whether it was, we will have our own conflicts to resolve and our own conflictual anxiety to address.

LIFTING THE VEIL ON YOUR OWN THOUGHTS

Not only must you become a meaning expert, you must also become an anxiety expert: someone who understands the sources and effects of anxiety in his life and has learned how to eliminate, quell, accept, and brave that anxiety.

Sometimes you work to eliminate your anxiety, for example by teasing apart and resolving an inner conflict. Sometimes you work to quell or manage your anxiety, say by using an anxiety management tool like personal affirmations, breathing techniques, or guided visualizations. Sometimes you just accept and embrace your anxiety, for example by exclaiming, "So I'm anxious. No big deal!" At all times you brave your anxiety, rather than run from it. Otherwise you will never stop running.

If you want to become an anxiety expert, you start by lifting the veil on your own thoughts. When you hear yourself say, "A novel feels too ambitious" or "A Mozart aria is beyond me," you stop and ask yourself, "Is anxiety making me feel unready?" When you hear yourself say, "I've got to cancel that meeting with that gallery owner—I'm feeling too sick," you stop and ask yourself, "Is anxiety making me feel unwell?" When you hear yourself say, "I can't perform in a noisy club," you stop and ask yourself, "Is anxiety making me believe that I can't do such a thing?"

Anxiety is often at the root of the common linguistic forms that we use in talking to ourselves. "I don't feel like it" is a common linguistic form, as in, "Sure, there were producers at the party, but I didn't feel like meeting them." Another is, "I can't think straight," as in, "I always feel spaced out when an editor calls." So is, "I can't see the point," as in, "I can't see the point in approaching that gallery owner—he doesn't know me from Adam." Likewise, "It feels too difficult," as in, "Writing a whole musical feels much too difficult." In each of these cases and in many others like them, what you are really saying is, "I don't want to experience anxiety, but I don't want to admit that I'm scared, so I'll disguise the truth from myself with this nifty bit of language."

The most common linguistic trick we play is the "yes, but" trick. For instance, we say, "Yes, I should enter that piano competition, but the best musicians from around the world will be competing." Or, "Yes, I'd love to get started on a novel, but I should probably take a novel-writing workshop first." Or we say, "Yes, I'd love to paint, but where would I find the room for a studio?" "Yes, but" is a piece of self-deception that is pervasive because it is so useful. It allows you to act as if you affirmed something when you actually negated it. You can tell yourself, "See, I really meant to paint." What you are not telling yourself is that anxiety stopped you in your tracks.

An anxiety expert asks himself, "What am I really feeling?" and "What am I really thinking?" Honesty and truth-telling are the watchwords. There is no magic anxiety cure any more than there is a magic depression cure. Antianxiety medication may serve you, just as anti-depressants may serve you, but the best service is the one you provide by diving beneath the radar of your defenses and confronting the reality underneath. Sometimes what you discover will frighten you badly; for instance, if you learn that you hate being an orchestra musician or that you seriously doubt your abilities as a sculptor. But even so, you have no choice. How can denial and authenticity coexist?

MANAGING YOUR MANY ANXIETIES

Creators are likely to deal with the anxiety they experience in ineffective rather than effective ways. Obsessive thoughts and compulsive behaviors meant to reduce the experience of anxiety are often the first line of ineffective defense. James Lord writes of the sculptor Alberto Giacometti:

> Early in life Alberto formed an obsessive habit which seemed odd, though innocent, to the other members of his family. Every night before going to bed, he took particular care in the arrangement of his shoes and socks on the floor beside his bed. The socks were smoothed, flattened, and laid out side by side so that each had the appearance of a foot in silhouette, while the shoes were placed in a precise position beside them. This painstaking ritual, repeated without variation each night, amused Alberto's brothers, and sometimes, to tease him, they would disturb the arrangement, provoking outbursts of rage. For the rest of his life, Alberto continued to be obsessively concerned with the arrangement of his shoes and socks before going to bed.

When you resort to rituals of this sort—when you can't help but check the front door nine times to make sure that it is locked, when you can't get a worry out of your head no matter how hard you try, when you wash compulsively or fly into a rage if your belongings are rearranged—anxiety is winning. Obsessions and compulsions of this sort are not innocent since the creator who is forced to resort to them is a slave to his anxiety. Unaware of the role anxiety is playing in his life and too anxious to confront his fears, he is trapped in a ritualized defense against what are largely nonexistent threats.

An artist may pose as the boldest, most self-assured, most self-satisfied person in the world. Yet he may actually be tormented by anxiety, so much so that he looks incapacitated rather than heroic to those who know him. Meryle Secrest described Salvador Dalí:

> He came to Paris in 1929, totally terrified. "He couldn't even cross the street. His only means of transport was a taxi. He fell down several times a day," Thirion recalled. He was afraid of almost everything, from traveling by boat to insects in general. He could not buy shoes because he was unable to expose his feet in public. He was the absolute victim of rigorous habit. Each day he ate the same things in the same restaurants and took the same walks. His ability to lose his keys and his wallet, and leave his change behind was already legendary. Whenever he went out, he always carried a little piece of driftwood from the beaches around Cadequés to ward off evil spirits. The fact that he could not even take the Métro was a serious inconvenience for someone on a limited budget.

Just becoming more aware of the profound role that anxiety plays in your life can make all the difference in the world. Creators who read what I write about the role of anxiety in the creative process regularly write me to say, "I never understood that I wasn't creating because of anxiety. Now it's so clear to me! If I just accept that I am anxious, I can get back to work." One reader sent me the following e-mail:

> I'm a creative potter. A painter friend and I have been reading your book Fearless Creating. It's been amazing, almost magical,

how the information in the book is helping our work! Taking your suggestions for working through the anxieties connected to each stage, I've found myself able to walk through each and every anxious moment. It's great! A week ago I was feeling really tired and weak. Realizing that I was having starting anxiety, I read that chapter. Just reading about how anxiety can pop up the second you begin to think about creating really began to strengthen me. The very next morning (and every morning since) I woke early with creating on my mind. Thank you!

It is crucial that you acquire the habit of bringing your mind back when, because of anxiety, it wanders off to an unwanted thought. Sitting in front of a blank computer screen, anxious because you don't know how to begin the next chapter of your novel, your mind delivers up a thought to save you from further anxiety: "Fido is awfully quiet. I'd better take a peek in on him." An anxiety expert, hearing this thought, bursts out laughing and exclaims, "I must be anxious! No way I'm getting up and leaving my meaning-making efforts."

Along with awareness, you need courage. Anxiety arises because you feel threatened. The threat is real enough, even though it isn't a tiger that's menacing you. You may experience a threat to your self-esteem in your conversation with a literary agent. You may feel that your career and your worldview are endangered when you attend a scientific conference where your pet theory may be attacked. You may feel primal fear when you approach a blank canvas. These are not insignificant or "irrational" threats. What is required, however, is courage. Just as you will go into a dark alley if you think your child is lost in there, even though the alley scares you, you can do your meaning-making work even if anxiety arises to warn you and to stop you.

Anxiety presents you with the chance to show your courage. Gordon Allport argued in *Becoming*:

> *Existentialism admonishes psychology to strengthen itself in those areas where today it is weak. In particular, it calls for a wider and fresher view of anxiety, courage, and freedom. It is true that psychology, thanks to Freud, has not neglected the problem of anxiety—at least the type of anxiety aroused by feelings of guilt and fear of punishment. But psychology has little to say about anxiety over the apparent meaninglessness of existence. Because current psychology is one-sided in its treatment of anxiety, it falls short also in its view of striving and courage.*
>
> *Existentialism admits all the evidence that depth psychology can deliver; it accepts the fact that opportunism and tribalism cling to our behavior; but it would also give due weight to the dynamic possibilities that lie in self-knowledge, in appropriate striving; and would allow for the finite freedom that marks personal choice. Stated in theological terms, the resulting estimate of man's state will include all the factors with which a modern doctrine of regeneration will have to deal.*

The mind creates anxiety and scares the body. Because anxiety makes us feel wretched, we try to avoid it by avoiding those activities that produce anxiety. But this is only the way to powerlessness and meaninglessness. You need to brave anxiety, not do everything in your power to avoid it. Paul Klee wrote, "He who strives will never enjoy this life peacefully." Inner calm may be a blessing, but it is not a goal. If you make inner calm your goal, you are likely to start avoiding your very best meaning-making adventures.

The facts of existence make us anxious. Our own thoughts make us anxious. Creating makes us anxious. A cloud passing across the sun makes us anxious. We are built to experience anxiety, whether we live on an African savanna or in a Chicago apartment, whether we create monumental sculptures or miniature watercolors. Know this, and be brave.

8

NURTURING
SELF-SUPPORT

In order to make meaning, you must be your own best friend and advocate. If, for instance, you want to write a novel, you will need to galvanize yourself, light a fire under yourself, and also acquire your own undivided support. This acquisition of support sounds likes the following inner dialogue: "I'd love to write a novel about Gandhi's salt march," followed instantly by, "Go for it!" If you don't get that confident "Go for it!" in response, you are unlikely to write.

Many creators and almost all would-be creators don't get that "Go for it!" response. Instead, they get, "It would take me years to do the research. Where would I find the time?" Or, "How could I keep track of such a project when I'm too muddled even to keep my checkbook balanced?" Or, "I've been so tired lately, there's no chance I could add writing to my other chores." Rather than supporting themselves in their dream, as a good friend would, they doubt themselves and deny themselves their own support. Maybe you create in a white-knuckle way, as if it were a painful duty. Maybe you only create sporadically, with intervals of weeks or years between your creative efforts.

CREATING YOUR OWN SUPPORT

If you naturally enlist your own support and proceed with your creative efforts like a pair of good friends on an outing—you and your self-support arm-in-arm—you are very lucky. It is far more likely, however, that you are self-unfriendly and reluctant to grant yourself real permission to create. Who will help you? Who will care for you? Who will sing your praises? Who will befriend you? It had better be you.

Jeri Love, a writer and creative healing coach, explained:

> During the writing of the early drafts of the memoir about my late sister's death, I had to resurrect a lot of painful memories and, although this might sound cliché, I never felt so alone in all my life. I relived many long-buried experiences as if for the first time because my parents and I shut down emotionally during the actual events. The first 18 months living with and writing this book have been a roller coaster ride between heaven and hell. I have persevered because I know that completing it is the key to my long-term survival. But in order to write this memoir, I have had to find and create my own support, and the place I discovered it was inside my own life.
>
> For me, faith and prayer were (and remain) the keys. I am a 13-year practitioner of Nichiren Daishonin's Buddhism. Through my Buddhist practice, I have learned the importance of conviction and what we refer to as a "stand alone" spirit. It is these two things that propel me on a daily basis to challenge what I think I cannot do. It is that same spirit that pushes me to reach out to others, to be an example of what tremendous power and potential we can manifest, no matter what obstacles we face. I don't always have 100 percent conviction about my own work, and I still have demons that en-

courage me to eat buttered popcorn and chocolate cake instead of write. Sometimes they win. Sometimes I win. The important thing is my ongoing willingness to challenge them and my refusal to accept defeat as binding when my demons do get the upper hand.

Paula Chaffee Scardamalia, a writer, weaver, and creativity coach, suggested:

> I think the core principle in supporting anyone is saying out loud that the person and her creative efforts have value and worth. But helping someone believe in her own worth is a challenging, long-term effort, especially when dealing with an adult. We want to believe it, but if we have been told over and over again, especially by parents and other family members, that we are essentially worthless . . . well, who is a creativity coach to tell us any differently?
>
> My client Joan is struggling with issues of self-esteem about herself and her work. I suggested she make a list of 20 things in her lifetime that she felt proud about. Interestingly enough, she prefaced the list with the statement that she had only one painting she was proud of and was therefore going to list 19 additional things that she "has used to impress other people," to save her from failing the assignment! And the 19 things were pretty impressive; some of us would be happy to have done half as much. Yet she doesn't seem to take any pride in them whatsoever. She almost took pride in one achievement—writing a couple of books that have not yet been published—but then instantly denigrated that achievement, too.
>
> When I asked her, as part of our first exchange, to write some affirmations from her list of accomplishments, she came up with five. None of them were stated in the first person; each was distanced and constructed without a pronoun. The one thing she took some joy in was when I asked her to imagine being on a desert island with no demands, no responsibilities, and the ability to make any creative tool or resource appear with a wish. What would that fantasy look like? She was clear, concise, and even playfully hu-

morous about it. She wanted three major museums and an art ware-
house with paint supplies and plenty of canned food. She mentioned
that she might grow tired of coconuts after a while but that she
wouldn't care if the rescue boat never came!

I believe she is going to require a lot of emotional support and
affirmation from me about her life accomplishments and the value
of her dreams—and time, lots of time. I intend to acknowledge her
accomplishments and admire her courage, commitment, and
strength of will. Then we can see whether we can move from there
into directing these traits into her work. I want to see whether she
is willing to reframe her affirmations and then paint them large
enough to hang somewhere where she can see them frequently
throughout the day. And I think I may use fantasy and dream work
to help her begin to envision a creative life for herself, something
we can help her manifest.

LOVING THE UNLOVABLE, TOUCHING THE UNTOUCHABLE

You may have calculated that the beauty in your life will reside in your artistic or scientific creations and that if you can make your poem, sculpture, or theory true and beautiful, you will have done a sufficient job of realizing your potential and making meaning. This is a mistaken calculation. Unless you can find the heart to call yourself the beauty in life, despair will pursue you no matter how many of your paintings end up in museums or how many of your articles end up in scientific journals.

Marsha Ellis, a writer, sent me the following letter:

For close to seven years now I've been blocked. I am pretty much
textbook in my background. I'm a recovering addict. A survivor of at
least 16 years of sexual molestation. I was forbidden to write as a child

and even had my writings ripped from notebooks and tacked to the garage wall when I was about 15. This was my punishment for my parents not liking my poetry and other things I had written at the time. Those pages were kept up for months and shown to anyone visiting our house. Mustn't this have something to do with my fear of writing?

I did keep writing, though, and eventually became a fiction major at college. I had a lot of success there. I was published in every anthology the school published each year I was there and even won awards. But then . . . something died. I remember this cold fear overwhelming me and it's been a slow death ever since. I often refer to my writer self as this decaying corpse clinging to my back. I can't shake it off and so everywhere I go it's there, festering and dripping and always whining and whining and whining. A part of me wishes to finally kill off this damn corpse but another bigger part wishes only to breathe life into the poor dear. Unfortunately, I'm still unable to give in. To grant myself permission to write.

How can you feel like the beauty in life when you've been shamed as Marsha was shamed? What sort of housecleaning will sweep away your self-doubts and pain?

Jan Worthington, a painter, observed:

I believe that most of the people in my family have been artists. Unfortunately, they have all been blocked artists. I think that the worst family situation is a family of blocked artists. My family has been marred with alcoholism and violence. I believe that these conditions have existed because no one ever knew that it was safe to be an artist. It seemed when I tried to be an artist, I always had to do or be something else. And it seemed that being that something else always took me away from my art, my love. I had to learn and be willing to see the fact that I am not odd or crazy or weird or insane or that if I practice my art I will be odd or weird or go insane. I was never willing to see that until I read Fearless Creating.

I discovered something else. Since I did not know that it was *safe to be an artist, I tried my best to punish myself for trying. It was as if being an artist was a bad thing. At least, that was how I was taught. It was not a readily identifiable lesson, but it was there all the time. I have discovered that there are a thousand ways to kill myself. The easiest are gunshots, overdoses, and razors. Being raised a Christian, I could never have considered those methods. The ones I chose were violent relationships, forsaking needed dental and medical care, dabbling in a humiliating alcohol addiction, wallowing in deep depression and fear. It is funny that people never mention those as attempted suicides. They are, but they take a little bit longer.*

When you don't experience yourself as the beauty in life, you attempt small suicides every day. Maybe you manage to write, paint, or compose. But your real goal for the day is to obliterate it. A self-friendlier you would look for the opportunity to please yourself, help yourself, live your life plan, act righteously, make meaning, and find joy. A self-friendlier you would remember where the beauty resides: in you alone. The beauty in a sunset, a baby's smile, or in the idea of liberty is not independent of an observer, whose inner sense of beauty must be activated for external beauty to exist.

Audrey Smith, an artist, reported:

I got a degree in business because art was not an acceptable choice to my parents. I began painting, but I didn't try to sell anything I painted until a couple of years ago. I tend to compare myself to people who paint realistically and who paint well, neither of which I do. I enjoy doing collages, but the main comment I got was, 'I don't understand this modern art stuff,' so, since I didn't sell any pieces, I just wondered if I was dreaming. At what point does one believe in oneself as an artist? It's very difficult with absolutely no positive feedback. And it doesn't help that my husband calls me a parasite.

How many creators feel like parasites? Like untouchables? If you are one of these creators, you have to change your mind and heal your heart. You have to tell yourself, "I am the beauty in life. It took a whole universe to create me and here I stand, fully human." The song you write may be beautiful, the research you conceive may be beautiful, but you are the real beauty in life. Your sense of your own beauty will color everything and bring you a measure of peace, even as your trials continue.

You combat what shaming did to you by whispering, "I am the beauty in life." You combat what criticism did to you by whispering, "I am the beauty in life." You combat what a sterile environment did to you by whispering, "I am the beauty in life." You combat what not being loved did to you by whispering, "I am the beauty in life." You combat what insecurity did to you by whispering, "I am the beauty in life."

You fight your fear of making mistakes by whispering, "I am the beauty in life." You fight your fear of the unknown by whispering, "I am the beauty in life." You fight your fear of mediocrity by whispering, "I am the beauty in life." You fight your fear of embarrassment by whispering, "I am the beauty in life." You fight your fear of taking responsibility by whispering, "I am the beauty in life." You fight your fear of complexity by whispering, "I am the beauty in life."

You soothe the sorrow of your unrealized dreams by whispering, "I am the beauty in life." You soothe the sorrow of your personal failings by whispering, "I am the beauty in life." You soothe the sorrow of your lack of control by whispering, "I am the beauty in life." You soothe the sorrow of loneliness by whispering, "I am the beauty in life." You soothe the sorrow of feeling insignificant by whispering, "I am the beauty in life."

Maybe you are an unpublished author, or one with a few credits to your name, or one with several successes, or even a best-selling author. Then one day you hear about a writer who has just signed an exceptionally lucrative book contract. If you are lucky and no strong emotions wash over you, you may be able to survive this meaning assault and continue writing and submitting your work. But if anger, envy, or sadness well up in you, if you suddenly experience the facts of existence as bleak and horrible, you become vulnerable to a meaning crisis and depression. Just because you heard a bit of irritating news, your whole world collapses and depression sets in.

Your very mental health hinges on your ability to comfort and calm yourself in that split second. Like a parent who hurries to her child when he falls, you rush to yourself with all the compassion, kindness, and wisdom you can muster. You forgive yourself for not earning that advance, you forgive your rival for his great success, and you forgive the world for granting him what you desperately want. You do this forgiving instantly, in a split second, before a meaning crisis has the chance to strike.

If you hesitate, all may be lost. The very essence of self-support is rushing to yourself to help. Rather than stepping back to judge whether you really deserve some kindness, rather than waiting because you want to wallow in pain and prove to yourself that the facts of existence are disappointing, you offer yourself that kindness without hesitation. Events that could bruise your ego and hurt your heart happen constantly. Each time, you must put an arm around your own shoulder, walk yourself away from the pain, and have a friendly conversation with yourself until you are distracted enough that you can get back to your creating.

FEELING SUCCESSFUL

Our depression is kept at bay at those times when we have a felt sense that our life is meaningful and when we are at peace with the facts of existence. A lack of success is a meaning drain on both scores. Even if we believe that our creative efforts are meaningful by virtue of the fact that we are walking a path with heart, going deep, wrestling with good ideas, and so forth, if our efforts continually come up short or if they meet only with indifference, it takes a very unusual person, an evolved master or philosopher king, to smile and say, "I find my life good."

Most creators feel miserable if few or none of their creative efforts succeed. This misery may be culturally induced and the end result of the humanist thread in history, a thread that proclaims individual effort and individual reward the natural goals of a well-lived life. Whatever its roots, this misery is a reality for creators who do not succeed. Scratch a depressed creator and you are likely to find a person who is not happy with her creative efforts and not happy with the fact that the world is taking no interest in her.

Since creators are likely to set the bar high, wanting their scientific ideas to be major breakthroughs, their novels to affect readers as they themselves were affected by the novels of their youth, their paintings to be the "next great thing" in art, small successes—having an interesting thought, writing a strong paragraph, mixing a beautiful blue—count for nothing or next to nothing. On most days, therefore, nothing feels like much of a success. Who wouldn't be depressed?

Many would-be creators are aware from an early age of the possibility that success is a rare commodity and likely to elude them if they pursue what they love. Therefore, they opt out of creating. They decline to choose the creative life because of the fear that writing fiction, playing in a rock band, or some other love of theirs will never bring them success. They reckon that they will be better off, practically and emotionally speaking, if they choose a profession that guarantees them some success. By choosing this route, they are doing nothing more unreasonable than trying their best to reckon with the facts of existence and make a good decision about how to live their lives. But there are almost always nasty consequences to this reasonable decision.

David Stringham, psychologist and creativity coach, related the following story:

> I recently found myself at a dinner party, talking about creativity coaching. A friend of mine, a project manager for a computer game company, started talking about how he thought of being an artist when he started school but then switched to engineering so that he could have less subjective indicators of success. For an hour we chatted about life decisions he had made, career decisions he had made, what was creative about his current job and his life, and what was uncreative. I think by the end he had a better understanding about the course his life had taken. He had been devaluing what he had done and didn't give himself credit for the decisions that he had made. By the end of the evening, he seemed more empowered to take an active stance in creating his life in the future.

Creators who choose to put success first are likely to devalue their chosen line of work and their professional efforts, feel bored, hate themselves for not having braved a riskier course, and live in the shadow of constant depression. What they learn is that by selecting a sensible profession, they harmed their meaning-making chances. For them, the essence of self-support is finding ways to invest meaning in new creative efforts, even though they may believe that it is too late to start and even though they are still made anxious by the thought of creating.

If you chose the riskier path and decided to spend your life as a creator, you have the job of feeling successful no matter what your objective successes look like. You must train yourself to feel successful, despite what your heart and the world tell you about your lack of success. No objective success will ever feel like a success unless you have trained yourself to feel successful and have acquired the habit of feeling successful. Evan Marshall, a writer and writing teacher, explained:

> Sad to say, in my years as an editor and agent, I have known a large number of novelists who have achieved the stereotypical view of writing success but who are not at peace, not happy or creatively fulfilled by what they have accomplished. In fact, they are anything but. They are perpetually unhappy, driven by a desire to be richer, more famous, to sell more books, to make their publishers love them more. If you asked these unhappy writers what they're aiming for, what it would take to make them happy, they would have no answer because they don't really know. They've never stopped to figure out what success really means to them.

A vital aspect of self-support is reminding yourself that success is not a measure but a feeling. You can wake up, walk straight to your computer, write for two hours on your novel, and feel successful for that day—if you care to feel successful. You can wake up, go to your day job, put in eight hours there, come home, and do a tiny thing in support of your creative life, and call your day successful—if you choose to. You can accept yourself, call yourself the beauty in life, and feel successful for having taken your side and not opposed yourself—if you decide to. You can make peace with the facts of existence, let go of your anger and sadness, and feel successful for having chosen life.

Creators who do not habituate themselves to feeling successful have no chance at success. To acquire this feeling, you must have a long heart-to-heart talk with yourself and convince yourself that it is in your own best interests to stop measuring success and to start feeling successful. Having convinced yourself, you offer yourself ongoing support by reminding yourself at every opportunity to feel successful: because you painted for an hour, because you finished a poem, or for no reason whatsoever.

What may rob you of the chance to support yourself? Depression itself. When you're depressed, you don't feel much like supporting yourself. The world looks gloomy, your thoughts are confused and negative, you feel irritated and low in energy, few activities give you pleasure, and sadness colors everything. Whatever the cause of your depression, the mere fact of it robs you of your ability to support yourself.

But usually a ray of hope remains. It is on this ray of hope that you must pin everything. It is by virtue of this ray of hope that you seek out medical attention and, as a great many creators do, discover that pharmaceutical antidepressants can be a lifesaver. It is by virtue of this ray of hope that you seek out psychotherapy, find (if you are lucky) a wise, supportive practitioner, and begin to repair yourself. It is by virtue of this ray of hope that you find the wherewithal to take steps in the direction of accomplishing the tasks I've been describing.

9

DISPUTING YOUR HAPPY BONDAGES

Addiction, like depression, is a meaning problem. Other factors contribute to addictions and play their roles in maintaining them, but meaning problems are likely to have precipitated the addiction. Restoring meaning is the centerpiece solution to the problem.

It is no mystery why many creators become addicted and why all creators live under the threat of an addiction. Since creators experience more meaning problems than the next person, they are also more likely to become addicted. This is true whether they are unknown or world-famous, believers or nonbelievers, male or female, jazz musicians or abstract painters. If meaning fails, an addiction is waiting to snare you.

The path to an addiction is as follows. You react to the facts of existence with a serious doubt about life's meaningfulness. In order to handle the resultant meaning crisis and incipient depression, you turn to a meaning substitute, something that feels "as good as" meaning or that generates "just enough" meaning. This meaning substitute may be anything from fantasies of glory and dreams of revenge to Scotch, Las Vegas binges, Internet surfing, or sex. Your meaning substitute provides you with some significant relief from your feelings of despair and acts "like meaning." Turning to that meaning substitute becomes habitual, psychological and biological dependence sets in, and your addiction locks in place.

This sequence is the opposite of a rare occurrence for creators. Tom Dardis explained in *The Thirsty Muse*:

> Of the seven native-born Americans awarded the Nobel Prize in literature, five were alcoholic. The list of other twentieth-century American writers similarly afflicted is very long; only a few of the major talents have been spared. In addition to the five Nobel laureates—Sinclair Lewis, Eugene O'Neill, William Faulkner, Ernest Hemingway and John Steinbeck—the roster includes Edwin Arlington Robinson, Jack London, Edna St. Vincent Millay, F. Scott Fitzgerald, Hart Crane, Conrad Aiken, Thomas Wolfe, Dashiell Hammett, Dorothy Parker, Ring Lardner, Djuna Barnes, John O'Hara, James Gould Cozzens, Tennessee Williams, John Berryman, Carson McCullers, James Jones, John Cheever, Jean Stafford, Truman Capote, Raymond Carver, Robert Lowell and James Agee.
>
> A closer look at the long list of alcoholic writers reveals that four were suicides (Jack London, Hart Crane, Hemingway and John Berryman), while nearly all the rest burned themselves out at surprisingly early stages of their careers. A few preserved legendary silences that persisted for decades (Djuna Barnes and Dashiell Hammett), but virtually all the rest continued to write, producing increasingly feeble works, a situation suggesting the relevance here of Fitzgerald's much-quoted remark, 'There are no second acts in American lives.'

Creators are prone to addictions because an addiction is an ineffective but tempting way to handle meaning crises. You find no meaning in your day job. Your novel isn't going well. The hard work of creating is wearing you out, as is the hard work of filling up your seconds, minutes, and hours with meaning. You feel at odds with your culture and at odds with your world. A drink seems to help. Many drinks seem to help. Drinking becomes an obsession; showing up at the liquor cabinet and the neighborhood bar become compulsions.

The void does not go away, but thinking about your next drink fills the void. Drinking fills the void. The messes you make, the self-recriminations, the scenes, the bargains you strike with yourself, all the dramas, and all the tidying up fill the void. There is something heroic in your struggle to break the addiction, and the heroism you might have lavished on your creative work you lavish on fighting your addiction. The addiction takes the place of your creative work; it becomes the thing you think about, the thing you crave, the thing you have dreams and nightmares about. It becomes your meaning.

Addictions are often "overdetermined." So many factors may be present that contribute to the rise of an addiction that the addiction seems inevitable. This certainly looks to be the case for rock musicians, to take one well-known group, and if we stop and examine their circumstances, we get a sense of how an addiction develops. What follows are 13 reasons for the high rate of addictions among rock musicians: The first 11 are the standard litany, and the last two complete the picture.

11 REASONS WHY ROCK MUSICIANS MIGHT BECOME ADDICTED

Why are rock musicians more prone to addictions than other people? All of the following might be factors:

1. Rock musicians love highs and start out using their drugs of choice to get a buzz on, to socialize, to loosen up, to have fun, to party.

2. Rock musicians frequent bars and clubs, play music in bars and clubs, and live a life that revolves around bars and clubs. They are around drugs and alcohol more than other people, and this simple reality contributes to their high rate of addiction.

3. Rock musicians possess a belief system that values rebellion and nonconformity. This belief system is the ground for risk-taking behavior. The rebellious mind-set of the rock musician causes him to thumb his nose at conventional ideas of moderation.

4. Rock musicians are influenced by myths and stereotypes of what it means to be a rock musician. Drinking hard and taking drugs are badges of honor and ways of conforming to the image of a rock musician.

5. Rock musicians live on the fringe of society, where it is more acceptable to engage in illicit activities. They even pride themselves on living on the fringe, so engaging in these illicit activities are sources of pride.

6. Rock musicians are poor (unless, of course, they become rich). Poor people suffer more day-to-day frustrations than do their middle-class counterparts. They use drugs and alcohol to help them forget about their poverty and their misery.

7. Rock musicians (like anyone) may have a biological weakness or predisposition that makes them vulnerable to addiction. For instance, one study on the relationship between testosterone levels and professions concluded that performers had the highest testosterone levels and clergy the lowest.

8. Rock musicians (like anyone) may display emotional problems that contribute to an addiction. They drink and use drugs to bind anxiety, mask depression, deal with childhood trauma, and so on.

9. Rock musicians are ambitious and have what Zen Buddhists call a "greedy mind." One face of this pervasive greediness is the need to ingest alcohol and drugs.

10. Rock musicians (like all people) suffer from anxiety but are additionally burdened by performance anxiety. Their addiction is rooted in the common human experience of anxiety and the special performer's problem of stage fright.

11. Rock musicians expend an enormous amount of adrenaline when they perform, and their bodies are saturated with adrenaline when they finish. High on adrenaline, they can't come down easily and take drugs and alcohol to help them deal with the adrenaline flowing through their bodies.

It's easy to imagine that a number of these reasons, separately or together, have a lot of explanatory power. But there is more to the story. The 12th reason why rock musicians—and all creators—are prone to addiction is that intense aliveness is itself a ground for addiction. The 13th reason is that the pressures of meaning-making cause us to seek pleasurable meaning substitutes, which we then begin to crave around the clock.

THE 12TH REASON

A person with vitality, passion, and energy—a person who is really alive—possesses roiling thoughts, big ideas, and insistent desires. These inevitably lead to obsessions and compulsions. When these obsessions and compulsions are channeled in a positive direction so that, for example, a songwriter is only obsessed about the song on his mind and his only compulsion is to get the song down on paper, all is well. Then he is creative, engaged, productive, altogether alive. But because a creator can only create for so many hours each day and because creating is anxiety-producing work that he may avoid altogether, he is often left with kilowatts of energy to redirect. His large energy, needing to be expended, barrels him headlong toward an addiction.

It is great if I obsess about my novel or my genetic theory. It is wonderful if I feel compelled to write late into the night or feel driven to arrive at my lab in the small hours of the morning. My positive obsessions and positive compulsions are nothing but the expression of my passionate meaning-making efforts. I should want to feel compelled to write my symphony; if I don't feel compelled, that is the equivalent of my taking no interest in it. While I don't want to obsess about my neighbor's untidy front lawn or about monster insects growing in nuclear waste dumps, I do want to obsess about my own creative ideas.

The poet and novelist May Sarton wrote in *At Seventy*, the journal of her 70th year:

> Perhaps the answer is not detachment, as I used to believe, but rather to be deeply involved in something, to be attached. I am attached in a thousand ways. The price of being attached 'in a thousand ways' is that there is never even twenty-four hours free of pressure, but this year I am clear in my mind that just this is what my life is all about, and what I have to learn (so late!) is to accept the multiple demands and understand that a rich life is bought at a high price in energy. If I can be wiser about not feeling so compulsive about everything, all will be well.

A person with all this life energy must cultivate in himself the habit of obsessing and compulsing in a fruitful fashion so that he works hard at his creative efforts. Second, he must prevent himself from sending his energy and his thoughts off in directions that harm him: toward slot machines, Internet sex chats, or the next bottle of vodka. Third, he must find a way to get a grip on his mind and turn off even his fruitful obsessions and compulsions so that, for example, he remembers while writing his novel that he has a child to pick up from school.

THE 13TH REASON

When you abandon your meaning-making activities for whatever reason—because it is too hard to make meaning, because you don't know what meaning to make, because you've made some meaning and want a respite from meaning-making—you court an addiction. Agitated, bored, you throw up your hands and cry, "Give me sex, give me a high, give me something!"

Colin Wilson, chronicling Byron's many love affairs with married women and young boys during the winter of 1818, observed, "Byron's chief problem was a simple one: he had no idea what to do with himself. He knew he found social life boring and dissatisfying, but what was the alternative? Poetry might occupy a few hours of each day, but he spent the rest of his time wondering what he could do to keep himself amused. Life became an endless flight from boredom, rolling in his carriage all over Europe."

Once having taken root, an addiction reduces your freedom to make personal meaning while increasing your psychological and physical dependence on the thing craved. The addiction begins to take care of meaning crises in its own way, producing an oddly satisfactory state of affairs: a happy bondage. The great irony about addiction is that, despite its terrible consequences, despite the guilt and despair that come from being out of control and from knowing that you are out of control, the addiction is still less of a problem than is freedom.

The bondage is real bondage but an almost happy bondage, for while you are addicted, there is no question about how to fill up your time. You drink and keep drinking, you sleep it off, you get sick, you go to the emergency room, you make scenes, you lose friends, you break bones. This, it turns out, is easier than sitting in the blinding sunlight and answering the question, "What healthy thing can I do with my freedom?"

There is a beautiful story in the existential tradition, "The Bound Man" by the Austrian author Ilse Aichinger, in which a man awakens one morning to find himself inexplicably bound by rope. Instead of removing the rope at the first opportunity, he spontaneously decides to become a circus attraction. The addict, also inexplicably bound to his addiction, finds, like the bound man, important reasons not to fight the addiction. While he is bound up, he is less free, but he is also less anxious. Bound this way, there are so many things that he can't dream of doing—so many powerful limitations!—which he experiences as liberation.

Linda Schierse Leonard, examining her own alcoholism and her thoughts on the relationship between addiction and creativity in *Witness to the Fire*, reported:

> *When I looked up the word addiction in the dictionary, I found a connection between addiction and creativity buried in the original etymological roots. The Latin for addict, addictus, means to devote, surrender, deliver over, or give oneself up habitually. Is addiction, then, the act of giving oneself over to something as one's master— be it a substance, object, person, or activity—so totally that one's entire being and meaning become possessed by it? This sense of being possessed corresponded to my experience as an addict. Some of the things we give ourselves over to in this way are alcohol, drugs, food, cigarettes, gambling, shopping, romance, sex, work, money, power and control. None of these things are bad in and of themselves. But if one is possessed by them, if one gives up one's whole being to something else, allowing oneself to be ruled by something external, one's freedom and personal integrity are lost. In this kind of giving up or delivering oneself over, one loses one's soul.*

The bound creator becomes devoted to his addiction and loses his ability to live authentically. He may become bound to anything: stock trading, *Star Trek* conventions, painting in a single style. He may become bound to consuming peanuts by the pound, like Orson Welles, who claimed to hate peanuts. She may become bound to planting flowers, like May Sarton, who likened her gardening to an addiction. When you want to train your mind over here (where the real meaning is to be made), but your mind goes over there (to a happy place of peanuts, flowers, gin, or poker chips), you've become an addict.

A HAPPY BONDAGE?

In actual fact, this bondage is anything but happy. Addicted creators do not react to their meaning crises in a pleasant, mild-mannered way and sit patiently, smiling bravely as their addiction ruins them. The addicted creator is a wounded creature who is made ferocious by his felt lack of meaning. Consider Jackson Pollock, as described by Evelyn Virshup:

> Pollock was said to constantly need stimulation and excitement to fill his empty feelings. People remembered him ripping headlights off parked cars, punching his fist through panes of glass, crushing a drinking glass in his hand, and breaking down doors. At age 25, Pollock voluntarily hospitalized himself for the first time for alcoholism at Bloomingdale Asylum. Within six months he had another breakdown and was hospitalized again for his drinking problem, this time at Bellevue Hospital. His sisters-in-law, who had to watch over him, felt that he didn't really want to be helped.

A well-known novelist called me for an appointment but missed it because, on the day before the appointment and while intoxicated, she fell down a flight of stairs, broke her hip, and landed in the hospital. She never called back, and within a year her drinking had killed her. Clients have crushed their trumpets in drunken rages or sold their drum sets for drug money. One client, a singer, lived for pain-killers; another, a photographer, likened his obsession with speed to "a Chinese water torture."

What does this unhappy bondage sound like? Listen to Bobbie Lee Pointer, an artist and writer:

> I started sex, drugs, and alcohol at around age 13. I did it because I was curious, bored, and I liked the feeling. I drank too much for years, and I've tried to be sober, but even today, many years later, I'm still fluctuating on the usage issue. If I can stay moderated to my satisfaction, I will probably keep using until something happens—like an arrest for drunk driving, more blackouts, prison, madness, etc.—that convinces me that I really can't control it.
>
> I had eight years of sobriety, but it was always shaky. There was that obsessive pestering that never went away. I think it took me about two to three weeks after I first began drinking again (in December of last year) to get up to daily usage. I've stayed fairly controlled, but Saturday night I "blacked out" (my third instance since I started up) and ended up doing something I found unacceptable and embarrassing. My son was asleep, so he was not affected—but he could have been. Still, I love the feeling of being high, so it's very hard to admit it's unhealthy.
>
> This month I've become aware of several people in my life who are on medications for depression and are sober. I guess that although I know the dangers of self-prescribing, I'm happier in "using" a little than in being on prescribed medication. My boyfriend says that he doesn't think drinking is a bad thing. Because the Catholics still use wine in communion, I can almost be convinced that it's a sacred thing.
>
> Last weekend, I told my A. A. buddy, Sarah, that I had decided I wanted to stay sober over the weekend and that it would be tough. I told her I wasn't even sure I wanted to tell her but thought maybe that would help me succeed. The most important thing I said was,

"I have not been getting joy out of normal things—I only get joy when I'm using, and everything else gets so annoying because I have to do it before I can use."

I told my young son that I was trying to stop drinking beer and he said, "Good. Your drinking makes me sick." I said, "I don't do anything different when I'm drinking." He said, "No, your drinking makes me sick." Well, I don't know. Maybe I'll try using nothing during the week. I'll use only on Friday and Saturday after my son goes to bed and no more than three to six drinks. I have no motivation to quit entirely.

THE ADDICT'S TASK

Alcoholics Anonymous and other 12-step programs do not use existential language or talk about meaning. But meaning is their territory, just as it is ours. You begin to dispute your happy bondage by heroically willing yourself to understand that you are addicted. You announce to yourself, and to the world, that you intend to prevent the addiction from winning. You relearn how to make meaning, and you stop fleeing from your meaning-making duties. You prepare yourself to deal with your addiction's cry for attention. Of course, you may not want to do this work. You may prefer your addiction to an authentic life. But the bondage you experience will not be a happy one, and you know it.

If you are not addicted or if you have not experienced the lure of an addiction, you may believe that you are not at risk. Don't be lulled into a false sense of security. Every creator is susceptible to addiction because the pressure to make meaning and to continue making it minute-in and minute-out can send anyone scurrying away in full retreat, away from the struggle and toward alcohol, drugs, sex, or some other powerful meaning substitute.

Be ready. Bondage can arise out of a clear blue sky. If you wake up one morning bound head-to-foot with a sturdy rope, do not murmur, "How interesting! I might become a circus attraction!" Others have been there and are prepared to warn you. Charlie Parker explained, "Any musician who says he is playing better on tea, the needle, or when he is juiced is a plain straight liar." The poet John Berryman lamented, "Quart of whiskey a day for months working hard on a long poem. Wife hiding bottle, myself hiding bottles. Murderous and suicidal. Many hospitalizations, many alibis." David Crosby observed, "While I was an addict, I didn't write anything. I didn't have the attention span or the will."

Do you hear a siren call to an addiction? If you're a creator, it's likely that you do. The call is powerful and alluring. A voice sings, "Is creating hard? Is existence hard? Enjoy me! I am your best friend. I am your salvation. I can calm your nerves. I can quell your fears. I can take your mind off anything. It's so easy. Just come over here." Now you *do* need rope—to lash yourself to a pole, as Ulysses was lashed to save himself from the sirens' song.

10

CONFRONTING NARCISSISM

The term narcissism is made up of two contradictory ideas: the idea of healthy narcissism, which is a core strength, and unhealthy narcissism, which is a profound deficit. As a result, narcissism is a concept saddled with conflicting meanings. In *Narcissism and the Psychotherapist*, Sheila Welt and William Herron explained, "Narcissism can be seen as pathology and as an essential part of development. It has been considered a stage of libidinal development, a sexual perversion, a type of relationship, a lack of relationships, and an aspect of self-esteem." Given this range of meaning, it might be better if we avoided using the word entirely.

However, if we do a good job of keeping our eye on the inherent problems involved in conceptualizing narcissism, and if we make sure not to toss it around as an insult, we can retain this resonant word and even build on it. Every creator is a mixed narcissist—part healthy narcissist and part unhealthy narcissist. He must confront and work on his unhealthy narcissism while reckoning with the meaning issues that his healthy narcissism provokes. Healthy narcissism is an asset but presents a set of real problems; unhealthy narcissism is a curse and presents even more serious problems.

HEALTHY NARCISSISM
AS MEANING CHALLENGE

Healthy narcissism is a synonym for high self-esteem, good ego strength, positive self-image, and other imprecise phrases meant to stand for certain assets that we recognize as central to mental health. Healthy narcissism is an excellent thing—a quality that manifests itself as confidence, a love of life, passion, energy, and other desirable traits. It is no bad thing that a creator should feel good about himself.

This healthy narcissism nevertheless can create meaning problems and depression. If I feel good about myself, if I want to express myself, if I have high hopes and aspirations—if, in short, I feel like I matter—I am bound to butt heads with the facts of existence in a way that someone unconcerned with mattering will not. I am going to tackle impossible projects. I am going to ask myself to think harder and feel deeper than I may in fact be able to think and feel. I will crave a beauty and brilliance from my efforts that will elude me a lot of the time. I will pine for opportunities that my fellow creators also covet and that each of us only rarely gets. As a rule, I will find the facts of existence arrayed against me.

I am bound to see many of my efforts thwarted, many of my goals unrealized, and many of my dreams deferred. I am likewise bound to experience these unhappy confrontations with reality as meaning drains, meaning losses, and meaning crises. I am likely to find myself hard pressed to continue creating and likely to sink into depression. For no other reason than I possess good mental health, which caused me to set high goals and want large things, I end up depressed. It shouldn't surprise us to arrive at the following conclusion: The healthier I am, the more likely it is that I'll experience depression, simply because I find it so hard to reach my lofty goals.

My healthy narcissism is problematic on another score as well. Reality will hamper me and disappoint me, causing meaning losses and depression. It is also inevitable that I will drift in the direction of over-inflating my worth, my talents, and my uniqueness. I may do this just to buck up my spirits or because I stubbornly refuse to fail, but nevertheless, I am likely to begin to drift toward arrogance and grandiosity. Precious little movement is required for me to move internally from a sense that I can achieve great things, which is admirable, to a sense that I am entitled to special treatment; from a sense that I have a lot to offer, which is admirable, to a sense that you have little to offer; from a sense that I must assert myself and force life to mean, which is admirable, to a sense that the world is there for the exploiting. If I possess good, healthy narcissism, that itself is a seed that often flowers into unhealthy narcissism.

INCLINING TOWARD
UNHEALTHY NARCISSISM

The more mixed narcissism inclines toward unhealthy narcissism, the more we say, in common parlance, that an individual has a "big ego." An interviewer once asked members of the band Aerosmith, "As well as the band was doing, why did you guys have so much trouble getting along?" He got a variety of answers—about the wild ride of celebrity, artistic differences, drug use—but none of these answers seemed to satisfy him. He tried the question one last time. Finally a band member replied, "Because we all just have big egos!" That was the answer that finally caused him to nod in agreement.

Because creators are mixed narcissists who exhibit plenty of healthy narcissism but also plenty of unhealthy narcissism, we get film directors who champion freedom and good causes in their films but who tyrannize everyone on the set. We get writers who are supportive of charities for abused children but insensitive to the needs of their own children. When we see these paradoxical-looking and hypocritical-looking behaviors in the arts, sciences, academia, politics, or business, what we are seeing is the contorted face of mixed narcissism. It is maddening but true that the very same person can be humane and inhuman, reasonable and unreasonable, honorable and dishonorable.

When a creator begins to incline toward unhealthy narcissism, he starts to display certain characteristic behaviors. Robert Spitzer provided the following picture of unhealthy narcissism reaching clinical proportions and resulting in breakdown and hospitalization:

> *A 25-year-old, single graduate student complains of difficulty completing his Ph.D. in English Literature. He believes that his thesis may profoundly increase the level of understanding in his discipline and make him famous, but so far he has not been able to get past the third chapter. His mentor does not seem sufficiently impressed with his ideas, and the patient is furious at him, but also self-doubting and ashamed. He blames his mentor for his lack of progress, and thinks that he deserves more help with his grand idea.*
>
> *The patient brags about his creativity and complains that other people are "jealous" of his insight. He is very envious of students who are moving along faster and regards them as "dull drones and ass-kissers." He prides himself on the brilliance of his class participation and imagines someday becoming a great professor. But people do get tired of his continual self-promotion and lack of consideration for them. For example, he was lonely at Christmas and insisted that his best friend stay in town rather than visit his family. The friend refused and criticized the patient's self-centeredness. The patient, enraged, decided never to see this friend again.*

Soon after he appeared at our emergency room, complaining of auditory hallucinations.

We see this same unhealthy narcissism in the young van Gogh. He falls in love with his cousin, and his passion excites him and enlivens him. He writes to Theo, "Fall in love and look here, you will perceive to your astonishment that there is still another force that urges us on to action; that is the heart. I feel energy, new healthy energy in me; as everybody feels who really loves." But his love is self-centered and unhealthy. His cousin rejects him with the words, "No, never, never," and van Gogh refuses to accept her decision. Rather, he continues to idealize and idolize her, which is one sort of mistake, and adamantly refuses to accept her lack of interest in him, which is a worse mistake and an actual cruelty.

If you want to explore how far along this continuum you may be, look to your relationships. If you tend to fire your friends and lovers or if they tend to fire you, if your relationships incline toward the brief and the dramatic, if intimacy brings more rage than love, and if your affairs tend to end, at the extreme, with you delivering your sliced-off ear, look to yourself. Your inflated self and your deflated self are warring with each other and warring with the world, turning you into an unattractive aggressor and a self-interested tyrant.

UNHEALTHY NARCISSISM
AND RELATIONSHIPS

Creators need to love and to be loved. They require intimate relationships, emotional and intellectual friendships, marketplace advocates, wide-ranging networks, human warmth, the occasional handshake, people who respect their work, people who care about them. They need love, intimacy, and friendship more than they need gallery shows or tenure, for without the love of at least of one human being—and the love of life that flows from that human love— meaning is very hard to maintain.

What prevents creators from forging simple, excellent intimate relationships? Many roadblocks stand in the way, but the most significant is a creator's unhealthy narcissism. Many creators operate in the world with an ego at once too big and too bruised, making it impossible for them to accept the reality of another person. Jennifer Sils, married to a magician, interviewed performers' mates and asked them what troubled them about their intimate relationships. Reporting her results in "Working with Partners of Performing Artists," Sils explained:

> Participants were critical of what they called the "narcissistic" or self-absorbed qualities of performers and how this often made it difficult for the partners to talk about their own interests and concerns. Clair shared her feelings on the subject: "I get tired of hearing actors talk about themselves; I'm sick to death of it. I'm unimportant when we go somewhere; it's like I'm tagging along." Elizabeth added: "I feel like what I'm doing gets pushed aside. The people we spend a lot of time with are all his actor friends and it's always about Hollywood and 'the business' and that whole attitude about 'Are you in the business?' It really drives me crazy and pisses me off. Sometimes I want to scream, 'Can't we talk about something else besides this?' "

Marlon Brando described this brand of unhealthy narcissism succinctly: "An actor is a guy who, if you ain't talking about him, ain't listening." Thomas Merton observed, "Love begins only when the ego renounces its claim to absolute autonomy and ceases to live in a little kingdom of desires in which it is its own end and reason for existing." Iris Murdoch declared, "Love is the extremely difficult realization that someone other than oneself is real." Many creators, because of their unhealthy narcissism, are unavailable for real relating.

If you manifest healthy narcissism, you will act arrogantly some portion of the time and experience some relationship difficulties simply by virtue of considering your needs first. Yet, you will still have a reasonable shot at intimacy and love since your healthy narcissism predominates. If, however, your self-esteem has taken a battering, if other people raise your ire or your defenses, if you have no way of dealing with people except by putting them on a pedestal or washing your hands of them, you will act arrogantly most of the time and experience perpetual relationship difficulties. Your healthy narcissism will have taken second fiddle to your unhealthy narcissism, and intimacy and love are likely to elude you.

Psychiatrist Glen Gabbard reported:

> One tragedy affecting unhealthy narcissists is their inability to love. Healthy interpersonal relationships can be recognized by qualities such as empathy and concern for the feelings of others, a genuine interest in the ideas of others, the ability to tolerate ambivalence in long-term relationships without giving up, and a capacity to acknowledge one's own contributions to interpersonal conflicts. People whose relationships are characterized by these qualities may at times use others to gratify their own needs, but this tendency occurs in the broader context of sensitive interpersonal relatedness rather than as a pervasive style of dealing with other people. On the other hand, the unhealthy narcissist approaches people as objects to be used up and discarded according to the narcissist's needs, without regard for their feelings.

In therapy, an unhealthy narcissist plays out his unhealthy narcissism by failing to connect with his therapist and by avoiding entering into a therapeutic alliance. The psychologist Julie Nagel observed of her work with an overly proud pianist who had entered therapy because of performance anxiety issues:

> I expected at the outset that Mr. B. would tend to avoid closeness in our treatment relationship at the same time that he sought it. His comments about his previous therapy in sixth grade and his lack of serious relationships with women foreshadowed his defensive tactics with me. His ambivalence was evident from his first appointment, which he missed without calling to cancel. He was 30 minutes late for the second session. Although we explored his ambivalence about keeping appointments, Mr. B. did not continue in treatment beyond eight sessions, which were punctuated with absences. He terminated treatment abruptly and didn't leave a forwarding address or pay his bill, thereby continuing his pattern of impulsivity, flight, and retribution in situations where he felt anxious and could not cope.

Relating must strike you as more than a nice idea. Ideas are cheap. You must actually relate well. Van Gogh loved the idea of complementarity as an essential life principle, in color relationships, and in the relationship between men and women. He idealized how blue and yellow could support one another in a painting and how men and women could support one another in life. When he painted, he turned this idea into reality again and again. When it came to human relationships, he transformed the idea into reality only once, in a short-lasting interpersonal relationship with a woman named Sien with whom he lived as husband and wife. Had he been able to heal himself and shrink his unhealthy narcissism, he might have made a match, experienced intimacy, and kept depression at bay.

MINIMIZING UNHEALTHY NARCISSISM

If a clinician looks at you and sees the attributes of an unhealthy narcissist, he will diagnose a "narcissistic personality disorder." That "personality disorder" label carries a special cachet in the clinical world: It translates as "watch out!" You are a special problem, not very open to talk therapy, difficult to work with, likely to skip sessions without calling, likely to confront your therapist about the wisdom of his ideas and the genuineness of his caring. It is doubtful that you are particularly interested in self-reflection, in locating the problem as somewhere within you, or in making a single change in your beliefs or your behaviors. Not only will the therapist expect you to terminate quickly, in his fantasy he hopes that you will.

Even the unhealthiest of narcissists, however, have their strengths and assets. In *Self and Others*, N. Gregory Hamilton describes one success story involving an actor who, hospitalized with a breakdown, makes the journey from wounded superiority to empathy:

> Bob strutted onto the ward, bragged of his movie role, sneered at the other patients as "sickies," set out to seduce the nurses, and condescendingly humored the psychiatrist. Even empathic comments he considered an affront to his dignity—he did not need coddling. When the psychiatrist looked at him during the interview, he felt challenged and had to do battle, proving his superiority.
>
> The analyst primarily listened and commented infrequently. The patient consequently did not feel discredited by attempts at help or by the offer of new insights. He did not lose his sense of himself or confuse his boundaries by projecting excessively onto the analyst. His unobtrusive analyst served as a self-object, as another person who serves the self's function of soothing, confirming, and regulating self-esteem.
>
> Over several months, Bob was able to begin integrating his grandiose self with his hurt and devalued self. He slowly gained the image of himself as a talented young man who needed to work hard at his chosen profession. The realization that he needed rest, orderly living, companionship, and compassion helped him become empathic. He no longer needed to project his devalued self onto

other patients. He could help them build self-esteem instead of ridiculing them.

It doesn't matter if you are the greatest composer the world has ever known, the greatest painter, the greatest intellect, the greatest soul. You must get down off your high horse, tear your enemies' lists to shreds, and stop criticizing and blaming others for your own failures. You must alter your picture of the universe and let go of your feeling that you are a martyred genius and that the universe is your nemesis. You are special; but you are not that special. You must matter: but like a hero, not like a tyrant.

Each of us could be disagreeable; each of us could seek our revenge. Each of us could look out for ourselves and care nothing about others. Each of us has it in us to incline toward unhealthy narcissism. You must learn, through painful self-reflection, that no wound inflicted on you in the past justifies you discounting other human beings. Janet Burroway explained, "We now know that Rilke and Woolf suffered greatly over their writing, suffered because they wrote and wrote because they suffered. But we don't know to what extent their respective partners, Clara Rilke and Leonard Woolf, suffered daily exasperation." The hardest part of authenticity is acting like other people exist.

I'm willing to bet that, like me, you're a mixed narcissist: someone with real assets and real liabilities, a measured sense of self and an inflated sense of self, a warm heart and a hard heart. What do you want to affirm—your uniqueness or your grandiosity, your freedom or your lordliness? If you want the scales to tip in favor of healthy narcissism, use the assets that your healthy narcissism provides and do all of the following:

1. Learn the idiosyncratic features of your brand of unhealthy narcissism. Is your characteristic way indifference? Sadism? Preening? Dismissiveness? In the split second before you are about to manifest that trait—right before you are about to dismiss a friend, react indifferently to a plea, compete just to compete—stop yourself with an heroic "No!"

2. Consciously relate. Make a point of caring about other people. Choose someone to love, to comfort, to respect. Give without a thought to taking.

3. Moderate your reactions in the interpersonal realm. When someone injures you in a small way, don't consider retaliating with a nuclear attack. Let "less drama" be your mantra. Learn to count to 10 or 100 as a way to keep from needless venting and attacking.

4. Feel, rather than steel yourself. Have defenses but know how to drop them. Feel empathy, compassion, all the soft feelings that might lead to tears or love.

5. Manage your ego. Learn to realize that someone else's success is not a personal affront, that you have as many responsibilities as rights, that coming out on top is a poor plan.

6. Modulate your selfishness. Share; give credit; try not to snatch what might be freely given. Of course you have hungers, desires, and appetites, but greed is not the answer.

7. Reduce your sense of injury. Haunted by old injuries, you may calculate every interpersonal moment as either a victory or a further defeat. If you do, you will get injured a thousand times over.

8. Practice ethics. In your heart of hearts, you know right from wrong. Wrong is lording it over others, indulging in cruelty, feeling superior without good reason, making people kneel so that you can see over them. Right is right. Once in a long while, it will be unclear as to what the right thing is to do: 99 times out of 100 it will be transparent.

If your goal is to live ethically, you naturally want to reduce your unhealthy narcissism. But ridding yourself of unhealthy narcissism has another important virtue: It will also reduce your experience of depression. Unhealthy narcissism prevents genuine relating and causes relationship difficulties. An absence of love and friendship negatively colors the facts of existence and precipitates depression. How superior and grand will you actually feel if you find yourself alone, disconnected from others and defended against others, always guarding against some slight or injury and looking to get in the first blow? This is a recipe for cold-heartedness and despair. No doubt you will remain a complicated mixture of light and shadow; eliminating all unhealthy narcissism is too much to expect. But if you can reduce it from a ton to a pound, you will have lifted a real weight from your shoulders.

11

REPAIRING
THE SELF

People are harmed by certain experiences like being shamed, beaten, ignored, discounted, tyrannized, lied to, stigmatized, and hated. People are harmed by encountering too many disappointments, rejections, criticisms, burst dreams, and unsuccessful outcomes. People are constrained and injured by the concepts they form of themselves as low, unlucky, ruined, incompetent, untalented, hopeless, inferior, worthless. People are likewise harmed by their very biology. Although we don't know with scientific certainty that some people pop out of the womb predisposed to despair, to withhold love, to walk alone, or to feel anxious, it is possible that genetic limitations predispose people to struggle and feel pain.

If we are harmed—and each of us is harmed in some way—then every day the knots grow tighter on the ropes that bind us. We find it harder to relate, harder to live, harder to care, harder to try, harder to be calm. We know that we desperately need repair, but what can we do? That question, it turns out, is probably the wrong one to pose. If you say to yourself, "What can I do to repair myself?" you are making a kind of mistake. Embedded in that question is the idea that there is only one right thing to do. It is cumbersome but much better to say, "Of the many things that I might do to help repair myself, which ones shall I choose?"

You can shrink this awkward phrase to the succinct, "Which of many?" If you hold that there are many ways to repair yourself from the harm done to you, from the harm built into you, and from the harm you have done to yourself, rather than one perfect way—which, of course, keeps eluding you—you present yourself with the best way to proceed. Our anxiety, impatience, craving for oversimplification, and defensiveness cause us to demand one answer per question, as if life were like simple addition. To heal, we must expose more possibilities and make a more genuine effort.

WHAT CONSTRAINS US

Psychodynamic theory has two important points to make with regard to our inability and unwillingness to do this self-repair work. First, it argues that a calcification of personality occurs early on, in the first years of childhood, and this calcification profoundly affects our ability to repair ourselves. Our freedom to look in the mirror is lost as we begin to grow into a rigid, opinionated grown-up. In no time, long before kindergarten, we have already become a victim of our own formed personality, psychological structure, and brain. Our calcified brain then holds us hostage in a vise grip of repetitive thoughts, feelings, and actions.

Nor can we even locate the damage just in the brain, so completely are we bound by the calcification process. The damage is everywhere—in the way we breathe, in the way we see, in the way we feel attracted to this or that experience. All systems are affected and damaged. We have a whole body, whole organism experience of being who we have become: the anxious one, the frightened one, the aggressive one, the boy-man who is angry, the girl-woman who is blue. Psychodynamic theory posits a second essential tyranny as well, the tyranny of the dark underbelly of the animal: our instincts, our irrationalities, our madnesses. It is the part of us that would destroy the world over a small offense, that would drop our mate at the scent of another creature. Even the well person and the wise person has this wildness and madness lurking right under his rational facade. All that darkness is in there, psychodynamic theory argues, notwithstanding the trappings of civilization. One proof is how savage we become during wartime; a second is how unhinging 3:00 A.M. can feel.

Biological theory offers up a similar argument: that we are tyrannized by our genetic makeup, our hormonal imbalances, our neurotransmitting idiosyncrasies, our unique inherited biology. The more we learn about the human organism, the truer the dictum "anatomy equals destiny" seems to be. To take just one example, one study reported that individuals with anxiety disorders had a certain genetic marker in 97 percent of the cases studied, while individuals who did not manifest them showed this marker less than 10 percent of the time. What this implies is that a person who is built with the susceptibility to be overanxious, depressed, addicted, schizophrenic, etc., must somehow overcome his anatomy if he is to repair himself. Somehow he must change his destiny.

What does this suggest about our chances of repairing ourselves? That we are not very likely to succeed. We are likely to make no effort at self-examination, likely not to seek out the help we need (including medical help), likely not to experience any healing, growth, or change. Unbending, calcified, protected by our defensive armor, unreachable even by ourselves, we are built to remain adamant in our opinions, live out our biology, and continue to suffer. Since you are reading this book, however, that must mean that you have retained at least a certain freedom. It is on your remaining freedom that you must bank everything.

In spite of these grave difficulties—and they are grave—people can repair themselves. Miracles of transformation and self-repair regularly occur. The part of the person that remains free gains the upper hand and demands change, primes itself for action, lets down its defenses, surrenders to reality, and actually affects change. This existential reckoning is a make-or-break event, like an alcoholic hitting bottom. While an event, it is nevertheless part of a long process during which the person repeatedly asks himself, "Down or up? Slave or free? Cowardice or courage?" This long debate, for the person who wills himself to self-repair, ends in a particular moment of exclamation: "Up! Free! Courage!" This moment is one of the few true markers on the path to human happiness and greatness.

TRYING PSYCHOTHERAPY

Which of the many routes to self-repair might you try out? You might try to become your own meaning expert, to systematically learn about the meaning events in your life. You might try to focus on one personality trait and work on gaining new confidence, becoming more disciplined, calming yourself, becoming more thoughtful. You might attempt cognitive work and change your mind about your nature and your future. You might decide to affirm love and rekindle hope. You might do battle with an addiction or with your own characteristic defensive reactions to life. You might stand up and make a new, altogether more passionate commitment to mattering.

The main thrust of your work at self-repair is simple to say: You admit that you have work to do, you articulate what that work is, and you do it. To overcome the constraints of biology and psychology, you will have to make this admission very loudly—it will have to be a shout, not a whisper. You will need a warrior's courage and a philosopher's patience. And you may want some assistance. You might want help with this self-repair work, and so you might seek out medical treatment (because antidepressants may benefit you), psychotherapy, or something new like creativity coaching. Let's focus for a moment on psychotherapy.

The central treatment goal of psychotherapy is to bring into conscious awareness important matters about which a client is accidentally or intentionally unaware. A good psychotherapist reaches her goal of helping her client grow in awareness by being present, joining with him, listening to what he has to say, supporting him, making suggestions, being human. She maintains what Carl Rogers called unconditional positive regard for her client and invites her client to try out new behaviors in the world. She is caring, compassionate, and concerned; she eschews theory; and she mulls over what might help this particular person repair himself. Sometimes she laughs, sometimes she is blunt, sometimes she holds her tongue.

Most crucially, she offers support. She knows that while self-support is vital, the support you receive from others is also a great blessing. The support you receive from friends, loved ones, peers, marketplace players, and the other people in your life is valuable beyond measure. So, she reckons, is the support you receive from a wise, humane psychotherapist. Even an analyst like Lawrence Hatterer, trained in the Freudian school where "support" is tantamount to a dirty word, felt compelled to assert that support constituted the key ingredient in working with creative individuals. Hatterer argued:

Supportive therapy is an essential ingredient in the treat-ment of artists. A patient should be supported in whatever at-tempts he makes to abandon patently destructive thoughts, acts, or feelings, conscious or unconscious, directed toward himself or others. Past therapeutic practices have sanctioned an overriding silence and uncommunicativeness to these attempts of the artist. This practice should be jettisoned. Therapists should support co-operative patients in their use of practices which accelerate improvement and that enable them to eventually support them-selves.

No psychotherapists existed in van Gogh's time. No one had as her job description "listen and offer support." Van Gogh received medical attention and counsel from a doctor whom he characterized as crazier than himself. What if he had been able to spend years in an intimate (and, yes, bizarre and demanding) relationship with an Otto Rank, as Anaïs Nin did? What if he had been able to sit across from someone who would have asked him gentle but pointed questions and waited patiently for him to respond? What if he could have vis-ited weekly with someone who accepted him, understood him, and painted a picture of self-repair?

Of course it matters whether van Gogh was in fact suffering from depression or turpentine poisoning, meaning crises or organic brain damage caused by too much absinthe. But if his problems were pri-marily existential, as we have every reason to believe, might not a meaning expert have helped? Whether that meaning expert called herself a creativity coach or a psychotherapist, if she could really listen, if she understood to what extent painting mattered to van Gogh and also to what extent painting could never provide him with enough meaning, if she could enlist his healthy narcissism and con-front his tyrannical side, well, isn't it possible that she might have made a real difference?

A COURSE OF PSYCHOTHERAPY

Susan Raeburn, a friend and colleague who specializes in work with musicians, provided the following case study. It illustrates some of the methods and language of psychotherapy and is a good example of how psychotherapy can benefit a creative person. The example is a little long, and you may skip it if you have no interest in how one psychotherapist views the repair process and works with a client to foster that self-repair. But I think you'll find it illuminating.

The Case of Parker B.

Parker B., a boyishly handsome single man in his early 30s, presented for treatment suffering from depression. Initially skeptical about seeking help, he came to see me on the advice of a drummer who had heard me speak on health-related matters at a music industry conference. He expressed fears that the process of psychotherapy would negatively affect his already precarious relationship with his creativity. Despite his fears, and since I could see him for a reduced fee, he agreed to start therapy.

At the beginning of treatment, Parker B. lived with two musician roommates and by living frugally, was able to survive off the earnings of his band. The band had a strong local following, playing a lot of club dates both at home and in neighboring towns. Two years before, the band successfully landed a major record deal. When their CD was released, it got minimal promotion from the label, despite a national tour during which they opened for a name act. The CD received good but not great support from critics and sold respectably. The label dropped the band the next year. Parker said that he'd been cynical all along and wasn't surprised that it came down that way. Of note, however, was the fact that his consumption of alcohol and experimentation with amphetamines increased soon thereafter.

Parker reported that his mood had worsened over the preceding six months. He felt hopeless and unmotivated, his sleeping was disturbed, and he'd lost weight. Upon closer examination, it became clear that a predisposing factor was the breakup of a relationship with a woman he'd been dating for the last year. She had expressed her unhappiness with his seeming lack of caring and wanted more of a commitment in the relationship. More recently, she had been worried about his use of alcohol and drugs. Similarly, other friends had told him that he was becoming harder to be around, that he seemed impatient and reactive. He said he felt surprised by this. He said that he did feel guilty about missing so many band practices and knew that his performance was starting to slip at gigs.

The beginning of the therapy was characterized by Parker's superficial compliance with attending the weekly individual sessions. He frequently missed sessions without calling, despite his understanding that he'd be charged for the time. He also initially minimized the extent of his drinking and speed use but did agree not to come to the sessions having used or drunk past midnight the night before. As far as I could tell, he did comply with this part of our slow-to-build alliance. The frequency of his absences declined over the first few months, and a clearer picture of his behaviors and history emerged.

Parker's substance consumption in the preceding year had escalated from social drinking on the weekends and occasional pot during the week to snorting speed on the weekends with subsequent alcohol binges as he was coming down. As he settled into our weekly meetings, he began to acknowledge the negative consequences to him of these binges. He said that he first started using speed from time to time after his record deal fell apart, and it seemed to help his mood with no associated problems. He thought it had a good impact on his playing as well. I advocated that he commit himself to complete abstinence from all mind-altering substances while we were trying to work on his problems. He seemed to find comfort in the idea that antidepressant medications could be tried if his depression didn't lighten up with some clean and sober time.

I strongly encouraged Parker to check out some A. A./N. A. meetings and as (luckily) he had a musician friend who was working a 12-step recovery program, he eventually attended some meetings. By the end of the first six months of treatment, Parker agreed that he should completely abstain from using substances and was able to do that in the next two months, after several brief "slips" on alcohol. He didn't fully agree that he had a problem with drinking in the absence of the speed, and was clearly not committed to lifelong abstinence, but agreed to quit in the short-run if that helped his mood.

Over time, the relationship between us deepened. When I failed to accurately understand and mirror him, these breaches were explored and repaired. I challenged his self-defeating behaviors and cognitions and helped him to explore alternative strategies to feeling better and getting his needs met, to the extent that he could begin to know what those needs were. He reported feeling less depressed, had regained his weight, resumed full participation with his band, began dating someone new, and even began writing new songs.

As the therapeutic alliance strengthened in the second year of treatment, the meaning of Parker's family history was more fully revealed, and he began to share my curiosity in trying to understand the origins and emotional functions of his self-defeating patterns. Parker had warm but vague memories of his mother, who had died in a car accident when he was nine years old. His stepmother was highly narcissistic and critical of both Parker and his father. His father was a kind but depressed man who was not emotionally available and who had never lived up to his own father's considerable material success. His wife angrily and regularly expressed her disappointment about her husband's limited ambitions and status.

In our sessions, Parker seemed to become particularly anxious when feeling genuinely expansive and hopeful. It became clear that he feared his achievement would somehow make me feel less competent, as though there was only a limited quantity of good feelings available. He could not enjoy sharing his success fully, as he would feel guilty, protective of me, and then resentful. We began to place his ambivalence about success and recognition in a context of his fears that he would humiliate and devastate his father with greater success. As he worked these fears out with me in the sessions, he decided to share some of his thoughts and feelings with his father, with whom he'd reestablished contact. The meeting was difficult; his father listened, but Parker did not feel understood. Nonetheless, he was better able to see himself as separate from his father's life choices.

After about a year of complete sobriety, Parker decided to see if he could drink socially. He understood the concept of cross-addiction and seemed appropriately cautious in his thinking. His plan was to limit his drinking to the weekends and the quantity to two beers a night. We agreed that he'd experiment with "controlled drinking" for six months to a year and see what happened. In addition to the control question, a second consideration was, of course, whether social drinking would negatively affect his mood and overall progress. In that he had no (biological) family history of alcoholism and he'd had an abuse rather than a dependence problem, I was moderately optimistic. We also agreed that if he was not able to stick to his plan over time, or if his mood worsened, he would get serious about A. A. and resume abstinence.

By the beginning of the last year of treatment, Parker's band *was beginning to do short tours. He'd successfully sold two songs to well-established acts, and he was receiving royalties. His traveling for two- to four-week periods during the next four months necessitated a change in the form of the therapy, and we scheduled 30-minute phone sessions once a week from the road. Despite the obvious temptations and pressures on the road, such as hanging out for hours in bars, boredom, separation from his girlfriend, graveyard shift-type hours, and so on, he was able to stay on course with his drinking goals.*

In sharp contrast to his initial presentation, Parker was able to acknowledge and express his feelings of frustration and sadness being separated from his steady girlfriend. On one occasion, he let me know that he even missed me. In consciously experiencing his current emotions, he became aware of the depth of his sadness over the loss of his mother as a child and his feelings of abandonment with his father. He began to understand how he'd shut down his trust and hopeful expectations of others and was able to share these feelings with his girlfriend, which helped soothe him. At the same time, his relationship with his little sister became closer. For the first time, Parker felt that he had a family apart from his music.

On the surface of things, Parker B.'s departure from psychotherapy was a by-product of his decision to relocate from San Francisco to Los Angeles to pursue the song-writing aspects of his career. His band and girlfriend went with him. After our three years together, I didn't really argue much about his leaving the therapy. We both knew that he was ready. He was not depressed, had developed his capacity for connection with others, had reclaimed his full range of feelings, understood his limits with substances, and his writing and playing were stronger than ever. He seemed to have rediscovered his dream and, for the first time as an adult, was able to feel good about having one.

YOUR PERSONAL MIRACLE

The story of Parker B. does not cry out as a miracle of self-repair. Still, it is. With help, Parker worked bravely on the tasks I've been describing in this book. He learned to relate: to his sister, his girlfriend, his therapist, his fellow band members, marketplace players, and others. He disputed his happy bondage with alcohol and other drugs. He grew in self-awareness and began to see himself more clearly, recognizing the large pockets of pain and disappointment that contributed to his depression and that made it hard for him to find life worth living. He opted to matter by commencing therapy, about which he had strong, legitimate doubts. In the ongoing debate in which each of us is engaged, about whether we will spiral down or rise up, say no or say yes, and manifest our cowardice or our courage, Parker—slowly, without drums beating or horns blaring—sided with the part of himself that wanted to live. He made use of his therapist's help to champion his own repair.

Can we brave anxiety, make meaning, and accomplish the other tasks that confront us, if serious psychological or biological harm has befallen us? The answer is a resounding "Maybe!" Some creators weather the most serious traumas, psychological wounds, and so-called biological diseases (like bipolar disorder) and, with help or by themselves, repair themselves. Others do not. For some reason—some intractable psychological pain, some inherited vulnerability, some structural weakness, some "X" factor—these creators find themselves unable or unwilling to heal. But others do survive and heroically repair themselves. They wager, against the odds, that they can construct a life full of meaning and hope. Though part of them is dying to, they do not give up.

We wish we knew why one harmed creator finds the wherewithal to repair himself while a second creator is unable to heal. We don't know why one is blessed and the other isn't. We wish we could say why one creator finds a bottom, sees another way, and rises again, while a second creator, his pain and despair for some reason overwhelming, commits suicide. We can't even hazard a guess. That, however, is the abstract matter. What about you? Will you do what it takes: make cognitive changes, endeavor to love, endeavor to create, posit hope, maybe seek help, above all make an effort? The answer as to whether self-repair is actually possible rests with you. Maybe you can't deliver a miracle—but maybe you can. Stand up, even if your legs are wobbly, and deliver.

12

FORGING
RELATIONSHIPS

The greatest obstacle to intimacy is our unhealthy narcissism: our egotism, our self-absorption, our selfish ways. Every creator has this enormous shadow with which to contend. But other obstacles also block our path to intimacy. One is the fear that intimacy will steal our solitude. Since creativity requires solitude, another human being can be construed as a thief of time and space. Thoreau remarked, "I never found the companion that was so companionable as solitude." Michelangelo explained, "I have a wife too many already, namely this art, which harries me incessantly." Louise Nevelson agreed, "I am closer to the work than to anything on earth. That's my marriage." Lars Ulrich of Metallica reported, "This is going to sound really corny, but my companion is the band. For a little while the working title of this album was 'Married to Metal.' Now I know why my marriage didn't work out. For her to wait 18 hours for me to take my mind off the band for five minutes and finally worry about her was just not right."

The very fact that one has a partner who is helpful and supportive can be seen as a weakness, as a threat to our self-image and public image of independent genius, as something to conceal rather than honor. Isabelle de Courtivron explained about the French novelist André Malraux, "Although there were to be three more women after Clara to share his life, a major retrospective of the life and work of André Malraux at the Foundation Maegth in 1973 contained not a single woman's face or name."

Another obstacle to intimacy is the hard time we have moderating our promiscuous ways. Since our passions and desires do not abate simply because we find ourselves in an intimate relationship, we are pulled to want more and inclined to call ourselves bored with what we have. Anaïs Nin remained married to her banker husband but had a decade-long affair with Henry Miller and countless other affairs as well. Diego Rivera loved Frida Kahlo but also had to sleep with Frida's sister and every other willing woman. Virginia Woolf lived with Leonard Woolf but lavished her love and her sexuality on Vita Sackville-West.

Basic survival issues also cause rifts. Who in the relationship will be forced to go out and earn the money? Who will do the prosaic things—clean the house, shop for groceries, cook the meals, fix the leaky faucet—prosaic things that are time consuming and disturbing in their own right? Will this always be the woman, even if she is also a creator? Judith D. Suther described the painters Yves Tanguy and Kay Sage:

> *Tanguy was the ideal male artist for Sage to ally herself with. According to her sister-in-law, he was "very Breton, very male, very attractive"; perhaps equally important, he was already secure in the Surrealist affiliation to which she herself aspired. Sage's appeal to Tanguy, however genuine, appears to have been enhanced by his knack for finding caretakers. Weary of the hand-to-mouth existence he still led in his late 30's, he needed money. An acquaintance remembers that "these Surrealists, Tanguy, Matta, and everyone in-*

cluded, were penniless. Most exciting, admirably excitable but all of them BROKE, and Kay Sage had the advantage of having some money and a natural generosity. For the Surrealists, she was a matter of convenience."

Career issues also provoke conflicts. Whose career will take precedence? How will the inevitable disappointments—the rejections, the criticisms, the prolonged periods of blockage—be handled? What if only one partner achieves success? What if the culture favors one partner over the other for reasons of class, gender, or ideology? Say that she weaves and he paints large: Who will the culture deem the real artist? Anne Higonnet wrote of Camille Claudel, Rodin's protégée and lover and an astounding sculptor in her own right:

> *During Claudel and Rodin's years together, Claudel did exhibit a few works, never more than three a year. These public footholds dwindle to insignificance, however, in comparison with Rodin's conquests. She remained confident that in time her talent would be publicly recognized, but she did not gauge how fully, in practice, any artistic career depended on institutions, social connections, financial self-promotion, and a strategically chosen stylish position. After her break with Rodin she became increasingly reclusive and paranoid and from 1913 to 1943 she was confined to an asylum for the insane.*

Equally problematic and disruptive are the countless personality issues that surface: the unhealthy narcissism, the black moods, the anxieties, the addictions, the sadisms, the masochisms, the rages, the enmities. Françoise Gilot recounted an incident with Picasso:

> *I told him I had often thought he was the devil and now I knew it. His eyes narrowed.*
> *"And you—you're an angel," he said, scornfully, "but an angel*

from the hot place. Since I'm the devil, that makes you one of my subjects. I think I'll brand you."

He took the cigarette he was smoking and touched it to my right cheek and held it there. He must have expected me to pull away, but I was determined not to give him the satisfaction. After what seemed a long time, he took it away. "No," he said, "that's not a very good idea. After all, I may still want to look at you."

You might think that only large issues cause relationships between two creative people, or between a self-identified creative person and a self-identified noncreative person, to crumble. But very often the issue that ends a relationship looks trifling to an outsider. These trifling issues matter enormously, however, because they bring to the surface large doubts that one partner or the other has about the quality of the relationship. For example, one client, a dancer, wondered if her new relationship with an actor could possibly last. While they were visiting her boyfriend's parents, he failed to close their bedroom door when he went down for morning coffee. Didn't that mean that he was unaware of a person's need for privacy and maybe even unconsciously hoping to make her suffer?

Another client, an actress, wondered if her relationship with her partner ought to be ended, since they had such different notions about eating out. She wanted to eat out at the $75-a-couple level at least once in awhile, but he refused to go past $35. Didn't that make him pitiful? Anther client, a gay photographer, wondered if his lover really cared about him, since he'd failed to get him the anniversary present he'd carefully hinted at. Didn't that make him self-absorbed and cold-hearted? These small matters loom large because they're the pegs upon which we hang our doubts about a given relationship or about relating in general.

It would be wonderful if we entered relationships already equal to the challenges they pose. It would be splendid if all that was required was finding the right person. But each creator knows that she brings to her intimate relationships a real inability to relate, real disturbances, muddles, and fevers. So she has a second journey to make alongside her first as a creator. This second journey is the journey to intimacy, one that she will willingly make if she hopes to reduce her experience of depression. Friedrich Nietzsche complained, "I have no comrades—no one knows when I need comfort, encouragement, or a grip of the hand." Many creators experience stone-cold loneliness, and the absence of meaning that loneliness provokes, because they refuse to do the work required to make them fit to enter into genuine partnership with another human being. This work is primarily deciding to relate, accepting that other people exist and matter, and choosing to invest as much meaning in relationships as in individual accomplishments.

YOU, ME, AND US

Jane Anderson, an actress, reported:

> When I was 19, in my first year of college studying to be an actress, I met an older actor. He was well-regarded and had lots of roles. We had been lovers for less than a year when he surprised me by saying, "I could never marry an actress. If we got serious, you'd have to give it up." I asked why, and he replied, "Because if you started getting better parts than me, I couldn't stand it." I told him that we weren't in direct competition, but he said, "That doesn't matter. If you wound up getting work more often, I'd be jealous." We split up not long after that because I began to think of him as selfish and unfair.
>
> After some experiences with other actors and performers, I thought I'd really wise up and date outside the talent pool. I fell for a man with a background in the arts who wanted to work for the

government. *We moved to Virginia and lived together for four years. He became increasingly devoted to his job, increasingly conservative, and increasingly intolerant of my artistic activities. I got lots of work, had an agent, did local theater, and was a scholarship student with a dance company.*

Mr. R. often said that he wouldn't mind how much time my acting work took me away from home if I just got paid for it a little better. I still had a full-time day job and was gone a lot of evenings. When I left each evening to go to class or rehearsal, Mr. R. would pout and say, 'I wish you didn't have to go.' After a couple years, the pouting became the silent treatment. He withheld sex (he was 'too tired' by the time I came home). He belittled my plays, griped that my agent must be a failure if she hadn't made me rich and famous yet, and insulted my friends in the arts.

He tried repeatedly to get me to apply for a 'better,' less-flexible day job, insisting that my work as an actress really didn't matter. Finally he began having affairs, and I went on a brief tour to do a show in Chicago and Seattle, which provided the break I needed to decide to leave him. A year later, he married an acquaintance of mine who is a talented sculptor. Since their marriage, she has stopped sculpting and works many hours to bring in an income that has allowed them to buy a house and a lifestyle. I've stopped thinking it was all my fault that the relationship failed. It was only my refusal to give up my creative work, which I think is my right.

Creators often conclude that they are not fit for intimacy, that the people they meet are not fit to be their intimates, and that the very idea of relating is suspect. They declare that human frailties and shortcomings put the lie to love and intimacy. Internally they deconstruct "romance," "love," "intimacy," "marriage," "family," and the rest of the vocabulary of relating and find only stale metaphors, hopeless romanticism, and wishful thinking. Experience tells them that intimacy is just another myth.

Van Gogh explained to Theo about his relationship with Sien: "The ceremony of marriage is not what would make Sien my wife; we are bound together by a strong bond of mutual affection and by the help we mutually give each other. . . . The feeling between Sien and me is real; it is no dream, it is reality." Reading this, disillusioned creators exclaim, "Reality! This great love, this splendid partnership lasted barely a few months, not 50 years! If you look at his painting, *First Steps of a Child*, you might be tempted to believe that he and Sien had a chance together. If you read his declarations to Theo, you might be fooled. But in reality he just walks away. So much for love!" Disillusioned creators find in van Gogh, in tabloid headlines, and in their own checkered histories abundant evidence that human beings rarely create excellent, equal, and enduring partnerships.

Sometimes creators primarily skewer themselves, as in George Bernard Shaw's ironic self-indictment: "I was taught when I was young that if people would only love one another, all would be well with the world. I found that when I tried to put that into practice not only were other people seldom lovable, but I was not very lovable myself." We hear it in the dancer Violette Verdy's declaration: "With my idealism about dance, it was insane to pretend that I could compromise in another area of my life. So I am not available for romance— except for accidents, which do sometimes happen." We hear it plainly in Sid Vicious's brutally honest, "I've only been in love with a beer bottle and a mirror."

Sometimes they indict the other person. Anna Dostoyevsky wrote about her husband Fyodor: "I even think that he is incapable of love; he is too much occupied with other thoughts and ideas to become strongly attached to anyone earthly." Shelley Winters remarked on her husband, "We had a lot in common. I loved him and he loved him." Tori Amos described men in general: "Guys would sleep with a bicycle if it had the right color lip-gloss on." Jean-Paul Sartre articulated this indictment most succinctly: "Hell is other people."

Sometimes the very idea of intimacy is indicted. Athol Fugard argued, "I do not know of a single relationship in my life in which I wasn't eating or being eaten." Paul Valéry declared, "God created man and, finding him not sufficiently alone, gave him a companion to make him feel his solitude more." François Mauriac argued, "Human love is often but the encounter of two weaknesses." Katharine Hepburn observed, "Sometimes I wonder if men and women really suit each other. Perhaps they should live next door and just visit now and then." And W. Somerset Maugham declared, "Love is only a dirty trick played on us to achieve the continuation of the species."

But intimacy is neither a myth nor an impossibility. It is a matter of attitude, work, and probably some luck. First, you need to come down on the side of relating and adopt the belief that intimacy is valuable and worth the work. Second, you must mature into a person who can love and be loved, who sees his own faults and tries to minimize them, who blames less and embraces more. Third, you need the luck of meeting a suitable partner, one who, like you, is principled and self-aware. If all this comes together, you may be blessed with a relationship made excellent by the combined efforts of two people who want the best for each other.

This is not to say that a good relationship will look conventional. Qualities of respectfulness, friendliness, solicitousness, and so on can and do exist in the most unconventional relationships. It is not the form of the relationship that matters, not the whiteness of the picket fence that surrounds the couple's house that counts, but the relationship's actual qualities. You and your partner may never marry. You and your partner may give birth to children, adopt children, or not have children. You may live apart from your partner for significant periods of the year, as Georgia O'Keeffe and Alfred Stieglitz did—she in New Mexico, he in New York. Excellence, not conventionality, is all that matters.

Lisa Tickner wrote of her parents, the painters Vanessa Bell and Duncan Grant, the one heterosexual and the other homosexual: "When Vanessa was timid and tentative, Duncan would help by being audacious. When he was disoriented, she would be authoritative. She would straighten out his muddles and laugh at his perplexities; when her self-confidence failed her, he would support and reassure her." This partnership, considered by their contemporaries the best in Bloomsbury, was not a conventional one, but it possessed qualities recognized by their peers as rare and special.

In a successful intimate relationship, you and your partner strive to care for each other's solitude, keep passion alive, gently exchange truths, support each other's dreams and careers, accept life's many difficulties, and remain best friends. The individuality of a creator is not snuffed out in a mature, interdependent relationship. Rather, it is safeguarded there. It will take two people to accomplish this, two people who are walking separate paths and the same path together. The obstacles are enormous; yet the only question is, "Are you willing?"

CREATORS TOGETHER

I received the following letter from a Hollywood director:

> I have been a director/writer of television for many years, am forty-five, and feel that this is the time I must break the wall between me and what I feel I was put on earth to do: write and direct GOOD feature films. I have been tremendously pleased with my current script, and with the synergy between me and my life partner/editor, Marvin. We both thought your notion of an "artists' group" in Fearless Creating was a good one and we have been planning to start one for weeks.

Being professional procrastinators, we finally just called
people Friday and set one for this evening. We had a nice turnout
of about fifteen people—all brought bits of food and drink—and
we finally gathered in the living room, a.k.a. "the salon," and
talked. Oddly, the result was less than satisfactory. We had an
Emmy award–winning screenwriter, four directors (five, counting
me), several actors (ranging in age from 60 to 20), and others in
the business.

We fell into the normal nosh-and-drink-and-network Hollywood
mode for awhile, then brought the group together and started to direct the talk in various ways, explaining the genesis of the idea for
an artists' group. We brought up some of your notions that have
helped me, such as inviting anxiety and managing it. I emphasized
your points about artists, about sharing, about support. As talk ensued, there were many individual issues—homosexuals in enter-
tainment, the evil that lurks in studio offices, and so on—but it
did not seem to migrate naturally into a discussion of creativity and
I was loathe to act as facilitator or make it too riddled with
"shoulds." In sum, it was a disappointment.

I would love to carry on this tradition of "Salons," but not like
tonight. We are obviously missing something. We both agree that
the turnout was skewed into the film/t.v. "industry" element, which
carries its own baggage in this town. We had tried to bring in
painters, musicians, photographers, etc., but none of them showed.
The group was also heavily slanted toward people in their middle
ages, which brought what one of the younger people called a certain "kvetching" and negativity to the conversation (we all have
horror stories down here). At some point it resembled group therapy
or an A.A. meeting. Several people seemed dismayed that they didn't
know the "purpose" of the gathering.

One of the people I invited is a young man I met on the Internet
while I was researching a movie. His comments have always been
very insightful and wise beyond his twenty years. He specifically re-

fused to come tonight and sent me an e-mail explaining his reticence. He wrote:

"To me, creativity is a very solitary and individual endeavor, not something that can be discussed or worked on in groups. It's something that comes from inside, a bit of the soul that is ripped out and made concrete (in whatever medium is chosen . . . sounds, words, images, etc.). The only other person I've ever been able to collaborate with is my partner—the muse channels through both of us, rips us apart, like she tears a doorway through our chests and peeks her head into our world, leaving us with something otherworldly, a tangled mess of sound for us to sort out.

"It is not something for discussion or panels, it's a spiritual process, my partner and I, sitting in a darkened room, playing off each other, bouncing vibes, letting go of the control of our conscious minds, so that textures and harmonies and rhythms just flow out . . . then afterwards, once we've returned to this plane of being, we're left to sort out the mess we've made. So I'm basically against groups. If you can present a coherent argument for your salon, a statement of purpose, what it's for, convince me why I should attend . . . I'd be happy to oblige."

I guess we are going to have to decide what these Salons are for, what people can expect by being a part of them, and whether they make any sense at all. More basically, I guess we are going to have to decide whether artists can get anything out of gathering together beyond bagels and gossip. I've read about the gatherings of the Impressionists—those weren't very pretty! And gatherings of Soviet dissident painters—beyond the drinking, brawling, and exchanging partners, what was the good there? So we are at a loss, wanting to try again, but not feeling optimistic that something deep or useful can occur when artists gather.

Van Gogh and Gauguin in Arles have come to stand as the quintessential example of two creators unable to maintain friendly relations. But is this inability the rule? If it isn't the rule, it is certainly not all that rare. Van Gogh and Gauguin were not very different from Dostoyevsky and Tolstoy who, despite being Russia's preeminent novelists, contrived never to meet. Elton John and Tina Turner bickered in their public rehearsals. Newton and Leibniz had terrible quarrels over who deserved the credit for inventing calculus. Unfriendly relations between two artists is all too common.

Creators often envy one another, desire one another, torture one another, take revenge upon one another, compete with one another, dismiss one another, jab one another, doubt each other's motives, doubt each other's aesthetics, throw up unnecessary defenses, and turn small misunderstandings into lifelong enmity. This ought to change. It probably never will, of course, but because it ought to change, because change in the direction of better relating between creators is a righteous goal for you to pursue, you have the clear responsibility to forge relationships with other creators that are as healthy as you can make them.

It won't pay to throw up your hands and say, "We creators can't relate" or "We creators have nothing to offer one another." You want to send yourself the following message instead: "There will be more meaning in my life, and less depression, if I forge relationships with other creators." Therefore, you want to cultivate relationships with healthy creators and exercise some patience before you dismiss the unhealthy creators you are bound to encounter. Remember that you can't hide from every unhealthy narcissist out there: They are in every dance company, every publishing house, every academic department. Rather, consider it your job to forge the best relationships you can, to be your best, and to promote the best in others.

Sometimes marvels of relating will occur. A publisher will love your work and champion it. A collector will become your friend. You and a collaborator will create a steady stream of excellent work and relish the collaboration. A compliment an audience member pays you will warm you for a lifetime. Maybe the hour you spend with a new acquaintance will help you maintain meaning for a month. Excellent relating does happen, and if it is rare, perhaps that only makes it all the more precious.

Depression is caused by the difficulties we experience with the facts of existence and the difficulties we experience making and maintaining meaning. When we find ourselves in a successful intimate relationship, both the facts of existence and our ability to sustain meaning improve. When we forge relationships in the marketplace, when we achieve friendly relations with a few other human beings, our heart hurts less and our hope increases.

Writing a poem may do less to cure your existential malaise than chatting on the phone with a friend. Writing the equivalent of the entire output of Shakespeare will certainly do less than fashioning a single successful intimate relationship. Creators know they should create—creating is in their blood. They are less likely to recognize that they have an equal need to relate. Cyril Connolly declared, "In my religion, all would be love, poetry, and doubt." We creators already have the poetry and the doubt; now we need the love.

13

MEANINGFULLY
CREATING

The centerpiece of a meaningful life for creators is meaningful creating. Creators force life to mean by investing meaning in writing, sculpting, composing, filmmaking, biological theorizing, inventing. They say, "Creating feels meaningful to me in ways that nothing else does." They are loathe to suppose that their creative efforts have ultimate meaning, that their poem keeps the Earth in its orbit, or that their mathematical insight saves the species from an asteroid hit. Rather, they make the more modest claim that this is the way they can opt to matter in human terms, the way they can fruitfully spend their allotted time, the way they can make use of their native gifts in an authentic manner.

Yet the meaningfulness of creating remains something of an open question for each creator. There is the suspicion that creating, like life itself, is a waste of time, a fraud, an illusion. There are the realities of the marketplace, realities that make poetry writing or classical composing feel like first-class absurdities. There are large doubts about the emotional payoff: about whether a novel, once written, will mean that much to an audience or to its creator; whether a line of scientific investigation, potentially fruitful but also extremely narrow, will hold a creator's interest. It goes without saying that creating is the best way—even the only way—for a creator to make and maintain meaning. But that fact is only a starting point for creators, a door opening into a garden of questions and conundrums. Consider, for example, the following observations from Sarah Stockton, a writer and creativity coach:

> My client Lucinda is a muralist who also works in several social service programs, working with teenage, homeless, drug-addicted girls. She tries to capture their attention long enough to get them involved in art projects, and she writes articles about the situation, seeks grants, and so on. Very meaningful work. However, the other day she happened to mention an idea she had for a painting that she has been itching to embark on but has resisted because it seems frivolous and not meaningful: painting a mural of pink flamingos.
>
> Now, the image of pink flamingos, when I read it in her e-mail, filled me with absolute delight. I don't know why: I have never been particularly drawn to the flamingos at the zoo, nor do I have one on my lawn. But the whimsy of the image, and her obvious attraction to the birds—their color, their silly necks—makes her happy, and makes me happy too. So we spent some time talking about how, for her, it is meaningful to show the girls she works with that life can be about play, and whimsy, and the silliness of these birds. Joy—that's what she wants to express. It's a wonderful meaning-making project that sprang to her mind quite spontaneously. I encouraged her to begin this mural, even if it didn't seem particularly important or meaningful in the usual ways she defines those terms. The meaning is there, just in a different form. She needed to find a way to make her desire to paint flamingos a meaningful one, and I think I helped her see that she was entitled to call her pink flamingo mural meaningful.

MEANING COLLISIONS

Abraham Maslow is widely known for articulating the idea that human beings have what he called a "hierarchy of needs," but it is probably more accurate to say that we have a "multiplicity of needs." As a general rule, a person will endeavor to meet his survival needs before his "higher" needs, but this is not biologically inevitable or historically factual. Whole armies die without blinking, young women starve themselves to death in their fierce quest for thinness, a man will stay beside his quadriplegic friend even though their building is about to collapse. If there were a true hierarchy of needs, none of this would happen. It turns out that our needs are not like rungs on a stepladder but like competing forces in a tug-of-war.

The same is true with regard to meaningful creative work. A creator needs to know what constitutes meaningful creative work for her, and she needs to do that work if she is to keep meaning alive. But there is no single meaning in life any more than there is a single need, nor can meanings be ranked any more than needs can be ranked. Just as needs collide—for example, when our survival need collides with our need to fight an enemy—so meanings collide. It can feel meaningful to write but not feel meaningful to continue writing if our writing fails to sell. It can feel meaningful to sell what we write but not meaningful to write just to sell. Creators are torn apart by these meaning tugs-of-war.

A writer is offered a book to write. Will it or won't it constitute meaningful work? Louise Sawyer, a writer and creativity coach, described how one of her clients handled this particular tug-of-war:

> My client Anna had a crisis concerning meaningful projects shortly after we started working together. She said that she was used to doing whatever jobs she could get, just to buy groceries, but that now she wanted to risk focusing on her own projects. In the

midst of wrestling with this issue, she was offered a $7,000 advance to write a book for a publisher she had worked with before. The problem was that she was not the least bit interested in the topic for the book and realized she would just be doing it in order to make money to pay the bills. She went through a lot of anxiety making her decision. She wrote me, "I know that the work I do is valid and worth something. The problem is, I get impatient and my evil twin is whispering in my ear: 'Just do the book. It won't hurt you. You've sold out before!' "

Instead of listening to her evil twin, Anna got out her calculator and figured out how much an hour she would earn if she worked full-time for six months to finish the book. Six dollars an hour. She said, "I'd be making 50 cents an hour more at McDonalds." So her reply to her publisher was, "No." That took guts. She recognized that there was a lot of grunt work involved in life, but she came to the conclusion, "This book would have been grunt work in the service of nothing I'm working on now. It would have scattered my focus and kept me from what I want to do, all for $6 an hour."

Since facing this crisis in risk-taking on behalf of her own projects, she has set up a business Web site, led a couple workshops, started a proposal on a book she really wants to write, and has gotten an easy part-time job in a gift store—which pays $7 an hour. It doesn't use up her mental energy the way the publisher's book would have done, and so she is able to still focus on her own writing and teaching projects. Recently she had an insight: "I realized that I have an easier time doing grunt work for other people. When I do it for myself, I get all bogged down and procrastinate—go on strike actually. I have started to understand that many of the preliminary steps to anything I want are tedious and boring, but necessary if I am to go further. All the necessary baby steps really do add up to something." I told her, "I am honored to work with you."

This tug-of-war is continual. We wish it were obvious which of two projects was the more meaningful one, whether a given discipline or vocation was objectively higher in meaning potential than some other. But is music more meaningful than botany? Is chemistry more meaningful than sculpture? Is investigative reporting higher than poetry? No objective judgments are possible. No one can assert that a rose is more important than a song about roses, that a knowledge of the physics of blue is more important than a knowledge of making blue skies with pigment. There are no experts, no measures, no way of deciding except as a personal matter.

These questions about what constitutes meaningful creating often tax and perplex creators. In which discipline will she choose to invest meaning? Must she choose just one? Having chosen a discipline, what subject area or subject matter will she pursue? Can she maintain meaning if she never masters her craft? Can she maintain meaning if people snicker when she tells them what she does, if her culture is antagonistic to her pursuits, if she herself is of two minds about the value of her work? What if she is positive about her choice but, because of her fears, her personality, and her circumstances, never manages to do her best work? Will she feel as if she has been meaningfully creating then?

A person decides that she means to paint. Will she paint flowers because she finds them beautiful, or will she paint dung heaps because she has a message to deliver to her culture? Say that she chooses to paint flowers. Can she continue to paint them if, in her own estimation, her paintings are poorly executed? What if she tries to say, "My life is a long apprenticeship, and I don't need any of my paintings to please me." Will that ring true in her own ears? Will that sound like a rationalization? Can she really live surrounded by paintings she doesn't like and find the wherewithal to keep going back to the studio?

Say that she chooses to paint dung heaps. Can she continue to paint them if, despite her masterful execution, no one will buy them? What if she says, "The subject matter of my paintings depresses me and apparently depresses everyone who looks at them, but I must create my dung heap paintings because I'm a cultural witness." Will it be possible to sustain meaning, even though the very thing she does to make meaning depresses her and her potential audience? She must also face the fact that she will need some source of income, probably a day job, since her paintings are not selling. If this is her path, can she feel anything but depressed as she walks it?

When I ask the creativity coaches I train to reflect on the question of meaningful creative work, they get queasy. They find it hard to grasp hold of an answer, hard to even understand the question. It is not difficult to point to this or that great work of art, this or that scientific breakthrough. Because you can point to these fabulous things, it seems like it would be easy to say, "Meaningful creative work has four legs, a head, a tail, and looks like what Einstein or Maria Callas does." But what about the Zen painter who makes a single mark and cries, "Done!"? What about the rap singer who glorifies killing cops one year and stars in a television series as a detective the next? What about van Gogh when he copies Millet? The matter feels too complex to unravel, or as if too many questions are being asked at once.

Yet creators do have clues and intuitions about what constitutes meaningful work. One will say, "If I follow a path with heart, I find the work meaningful." A second will say, "If I maintain high purpose, I choose well." A third will say, "All I have to remember is to go deep." A fourth will say, "If I maintain a real connection to my own thoughts and feelings, I don't go astray." A fifth will say, "When I find a good idea to chew on, everything else falls into place." A sixth will say, "If I risk a genuine encounter with the work, I invariably create something that I find meaningful."

A PATH WITH HEART

The answer I get most frequently to the question "What constitutes meaningful creative work to you?" is some variation of "working soulfully" or "taking a path with heart." Melissa Padgett, an artist, teacher, and creativity coach, related the following story:

> A client of mine has much turmoil in her life right now. She's researching where to move and doesn't have much money. She has a great ability to gather data and facts and is trying to decide if she should fly or take a train to explore New Orleans; or wait until she gives notice; or take a train or plane to explore New Orleans and then venture further on and explore Florida; or maybe include North Carolina in her explorations; and so on.
>
> She was drowning in ticket info, flight and hotel costs, rental car schedules, time away from work, travel with her eight-year-old, weighing, analyzing, sorting, agonizing, wondering if she really should or shouldn't do any of this, driving herself (and me) crazy trying to find the "right" answer. I hung in there for a while because these decisions aren't easy, and comparing data can be helpful.
>
> But without the meaning, comparing data meant nothing. What was missing for her was a guiding light to illuminate the meaningful path, to help her know the right answer. If all her data bits were iron shavings, then meaning was the true north needed to align them. And her true north had apparently gone south. Just in time, in one of those moments a coach sometimes gets, I remembered a quote from The Teachings of Don Juan by Carlos Castaneda. Carlos asked of Don Juan, "What is my right path?" and Don Juan replied to the effect, "All paths are the same; they end up in the same place. What is important is to ask yourself, 'Does this path have a heart?' If the answer is 'yes,' then that is the right path for you."

The quote had an extraordinary effect. Just like that, she stopped focusing on data bits and got inspired. She said, "Oh yes! I need to remember the magic in the world. The path with heart is full of magic for me." She began to remember times when she had made decisions using her heart, and how happy and free she'd felt. She was truly excited to be connected to something bigger, more bountiful, and more meaningful than mere comparative data.

Ana Garcia, a bead artist, explained:

If a judge does not accept my sculpture into a juried competition, I feel disappointed. But that does not mean that the piece has no merit. For instance, I received a harsh critique of one of my sculptures, only to have it highly praised a few months later in another show. I must trust my subjective understanding of each piece and my own belief about whether it has integrity. If it has integrity, I consider it meaningful. I used to think that only I knew if a piece had a soul, but now I believe that only I know if it carries a piece of my soul.

Whether believer or nonbeliever, creators regularly experience something they are likely to call "soulfulness" when they fully engage in the creative process. This feeling is the gauge by which they judge whether they are creating meaningfully. Even if the finished product—the idea, the theory, the composition, the novel, the invention, the painting—turns out flawed or not to their liking, they are unlikely to doubt that they spent their time meaningfully. The outcome, while important, is not the real measure. The measure is the feeling that they visited a region where connections got made.

Judging the meaningfulness of one's creative efforts by its felt sense of soulfulness is a point of view that creators consistently express. If the creator is not a believer, she may bring up soul or spirit reluctantly or ironically. If she is a believer, she will sound devout and sincere. But whether ironic or sincere, dubious or devout, creators of every stripe feel compelled to make use of metaphors, analogies, and allusions of a spiritual sort. The following are 20 characteristic expressions:

♦ Ingmar Bergman: "In my opinion, art lost its basic creative drive the moment it was separated from worship."

♦ Lenore Tawney: "I remember my first ecstatic experience, working all day on a sculpture."

♦ Wassily Kandinsky: "The word 'composition' moved me spiritually and I made it my aim in life to paint a 'composition.'"

♦ Jean Anouilh: "Beauty is one of the rare things that do not lead to doubt of God."

♦ Joan Miró: "Art class was like a religious ceremony for me. I would wash my hands carefully before touching paper or pencils. The instruments of work were sacred objects to me."

♦ Aleksandr Solzhenitsyn: "Art thaws even the frozen, darkened soul, opening it to lofty spiritual experience."

♦ Lindsey Buckingham: "Someone else's anchor could be going to church. The anchor for me is when I work on my own and get very close to something."

♦ Pyotr Ilich Tchaikovsky: "Composing is a sort of confession of the soul in music."

♦ René Magritte: "Art evokes the mystery without which the world would not exist."

♦ Ward Beecher: "Every artist dips his brush into his own soul and paints his own nature into his pictures."

◆ Peter Gabriel: "The spiritual power of music comes from the fact that it plugs directly into the soul."

◆ Otto Rank: "Art unquestionably has an end, but its ends are not concrete and practical. They are abstract and spiritual."

◆ André Gide: "Art is a collaboration between God and the artist, and the less the artist does the better."

◆ Aaron Copland: "The greatest moments of the human spirit may be deduced from the greatest moments in music."

◆ Tim Wengerd: "I believe the art of dance is something that brings people close to the gods. I think the body is divine."

◆ Henri Matisse: "I have always wanted to inscribe a spiritual space."

◆ Max Beckmann: "All important things in art have always originated from the deepest feeling about the mystery of Being."

◆ Le Corbusier: "When man creates a work of art, he has the feeling of acting like a god."

◆ Bernard Leach: "The virtues of a pot are derived from the familiar virtues of life and the breathing of the Universal in the particular."

◆ Jacques Maritain: "Art resides in the soul and is a certain perfection of soul."

For some, this has everything to do with gods. For others, it has nothing to do with gods. As Mircea Eliade put it, "The great majority of artists do not seem to have 'faith' in the traditional sense. But the sacred is present in their works." It is naturally suspect to judge the meaningfulness of what we do by a feeling that is as likely a brain event as it is communion with gods. But if we are to force life to mean, and if we are to use our human apparatus to do the judging, brain events are exactly what we must use. We can call what we experience soulfulness, if we like, and the pursuit of this soulfulness "taking a path with heart." Such a route to meaning is no more suspect than any other and has the virtue of being the felt experience of all creators.

DEPTH AND HIGH PURPOSE

In addition to conceptualizing meaningful creating as soulful work along a path with heart, creators also characterize it as deep work. Rosemary Warden, writer and creativity coach, described her experience of learning to go deep as follows:

> I thought the book I planned to write was a meaningful creative project. Certainly my intellect thought so. So I gathered my ideas, created an outline and schedule, and embarked on the writing. But day after day, every time I wrote, I felt like I was stuck in molasses. The writing would hardly move. Every day was another miserable struggle to get anywhere with it. I suspected that I was trying to fit the writing into a form that wasn't right for it but couldn't think how else to proceed.
>
> Feeling very frustrated, I asked myself before going to bed each night what the problem was. Finally the answer came: "You're staying too much on the surface. Go deeper." Deeper? I thought I had been doing deep writing: stilling myself, affirming my intent to go deep. So I thought, Well, I'll try going even deeper then. When I next sat down to write, I said to myself, "I'm going to write from an even deeper place."
>
> When I did go deeper, I felt suspended, hanging there in darkness, not getting anywhere, not feeling any inner impulse for the writing. Not knowing what else to do, I just kept sitting there, staying in that deeper place, hanging and waiting. Then after a minute or two (though it felt much longer than that!), finally it

came—just three words, but enough for me to grab the new idea by the tail and pull out the rest. Out of that writing session came a new frame and structure for the project, not at all the straightforward nonfiction style that I had thought appropriate previously. The project now called for more of a creative nonfiction style, a combination of narrative and nonfiction elements.

As a result of this experience, I am now trying out this new (for me) approach to my creative work: Show up, go deeper than I have in the past, keep my inner senses alert, and then write. I've written up my new process with a set of steps, printed it out on a half-sheet, and propped it up where I can see it when I write. This change feels not so much like "intellect versus intuition" but more like inviting my intellect to a deeper level than it usually intends to go, then asking it to partner with what emerges at that deeper level.

For the past few days, each writing session has felt like a practice at writing very deeply using my new approach. One session even went very smoothly, to my surprise. Whenever I feel stuck now, I look at the half-sheet with my steps outlined on it. I feel much relieved to feel more on course now with this project. It feels more meaningful to work on. When I went through this struggle with the project, I wasn't thinking that it was a struggle about meaning. But looking back on it now, I think that it was. For this project, I needed to go deeper with it to create new meaning.

"Operating with high purpose" is another phrase that creators use to express their sense of what constitutes meaningful creating. We operate with high purpose in order to live according to our ethical principles. We can be anthropologists with high purpose, singers with high purpose, lawyers with high purpose. If our creative efforts feel imbued with ethical force, if our products seem to rise to a level that matches our ideals and our principles, these are clues that we are operating with high purpose. When we operate this way, we are likely to experience our efforts as meaningful.

Helen-Anne Ross, an actress, musician, and creativity coach in the Netherlands, expressed this idea in the following way:

> My work feels meaningful to me when I feel I am doing something that expresses who I intrinsically am. It gives me a heightened feeling of being in a context. Often it has an element of social service—gifts to others—but not always. Nor does it have to be work that I do alone. At the moment I am doing weeks of rehearsal on a recently composed opera about Creon and Oedipus Rex. I had to travel to the other end of Holland nearly every day this week—six hours of travel a day. I have a very small acting part and have to speak as if I am singing. The music is very difficult, and the singers are getting very depressed. But my heart sings, although I am terrified that I won't be good enough. The whole world seems more intense, more meaningful. I see the myth underlying everyday things. There is a context, a discipline, and a high artistic purpose, and I am working together with others in a pleasant way. These are the elements that give my work meaning.

AUTHENTIC RELATIONSHIP AND GOOD IDEAS

Creators also experience a connection between authentic relating and meaningful creating. A creator strives to enter into authentic relationship with herself and demand of herself that she think hard and feel deeply. She strives to enter into authentic relationship with her creative work, hoping to lavish on it her care, attention, good will, compassion, and brilliance. She strives to enter into authentic relationship with the world, willing herself to stand up for principles and to lead by creating.

Becky Short, an artist and creativity coach, observed:

> *What does "meaningful work" mean to me? Connection. I feel that I am creating meaningful work when I make a connection within myself and with others. For example, I have a lifetime of journal writing that I am now gleaning from and shaping into a meaningful novel of connections—my personal life, my spiritual home (a coastal island), the historical past, and mythic themes. As I plan and plot and pull the pieces together, I make connection after connection and create meaning out of seemingly unconnected and meaningless events.*
>
> *Another example: The students I have been privileged to teach online and the members of my online writing groups continually remind me that by connecting with them through the writing process, meaning is created in my life and in theirs. What we are each doing in our own worlds has a profound effect on others in the form of encouragement, motivation, support, and inspiration. In my opinion, that is meaningful work.*

Thinking and meaningful creating are also connected. Ideas are the coalesced bits that creators chew on and elaborate into the books, sculptures, scores, theories, and inventions that we associate with the creative process and the creative person. You feel as if you are doing meaningful work if you are chewing on interesting ideas. Creators need ideas and, in order to have ideas, cultivate an awareness state that facilitates thinking. Tchaikovsky reported:

> *Generally speaking, the germ of a future composition comes suddenly and unexpectedly. If the soil is ready—that is to say, if the disposition for work is there—it takes root with extraordinary force and rapidity, shoots up through the earth, puts forth*

branches, leaves, and, finally, blossoms. I cannot define the creative process in any other way than by this simile. The great difficulty is that the germ must appear at a favorable moment, the rest goes of itself. It would be vain to try to put into words that immeasurable sense of bliss which comes over me directly after a new idea awakens in me and begins to assume a definite form. I forget everything and behave like a madman. Everything within me starts pulsing and quivering; hardly have I begun the sketch ere one thought follows another.

In most creative disciplines, powerful ideas are a necessity. If yours is a discipline that requires that you think hard, and if for some reason you fear thinking or if you are unlucky enough not to have any good ideas come to you, it's unlikely that your creative efforts will feel meaningful to you. When, for instance, a scientist goes for years without generating an idea that she herself deems inspiring and worth investigating, she is bound to feel depressed and even defeated. As the Nobel Prize–winning physicist Richard Feynman explained:

When I was at Princeton in the 1940s I could see what happened to those great minds at the Institute for Advanced Study, who had been specially selected for their tremendous brains. They sat in lovely houses by the woods with no classes to teach. Those poor bastards were not getting any ideas. I believe that in a situation like that, a kind of guilt or depression worms inside of you, and you begin to worry about not getting ideas. In any thinking process there are moments when you've got wonderful ideas. And then there are the longer periods when not much is coming to you. You're not getting any ideas, and if you're doing nothing at all, it drives you nuts!

The painter who paints her mountains blue and her trees yellow is operating from an "idea" of what her painting ought to do.

So, too, is the painter who paints Christ urinating, who demands photo-realism from her work, who paints gorgeous sunsets whose gorgeousness is a function of pollution, who paints distorted Disney characters one day and men with bolts protruding from their heads the next. These creators are making personal meaning by generating ideas, working with ideas, playing with ideas, and living a life of ideas.

ENCOUNTER PRECEDES MEANING

Many creators would say that a corollary to the famous existential dictum that existence precedes essence is that the creative encounter precedes meaning. You can think about meaning in the abstract all you want, you can imagine that landscape paintings or writing about your grandfather will prove meaningful, but no actual meaning is made until you begin to create. The meaning we intend to make becomes known to us only by virtue of the work we do in the creative moment, not from idle speculation about what constitutes meaning.

Accordingly, a creator need not plague herself with questions like "What should I create?" or "Why should I create this and not that?" Rather, she should make the basic choice to create something, using her best intuition as to where and how to start, and then simply do her creative work. First we embark on our novel, then we learn if we have chosen a meaningful subject. First we dig into evolutionary psychology, then we can decide if the field is interesting. Meaningful creating, in this view, is getting down to your creative work and making meaning in real time.

Mun Ying, a screenwriter and creativity coach, observed:

> I make too much of "meaning" and project onto it too many expectations, especially that it will be the "magical" thing that makes my life better. I forget that meaning is made in working, in my in-

teractions with the work, and not vice versa. There is a real price to
pay for confronting reality and letting meaning make itself known
as I work: I use up a lot of energy and often develop "allergic reactions" from the intensive immersion process. Things become scary,
brittle, too daunting to face. But meaning can't be made any other
way. Meaning arises as I create and as I confront myself in the creative moment. That's the only way.

If you work soulfully and follow a path with heart, if you go deep
and maintain a high purpose, if you enter into the right relationship
with yourself and with your work, if you nurture and cultivate ideas,
and if you risk encounters with your work, you are likely to feel that
you are creating meaningfully. These metaphorical instructions are
not like blueprints or schematic drawings, but I suspect that you
know what I mean and agree with me about their importance.

14

TAKING ACTION

There is no meaning without action. I have used the phrases "making meaning" and "forcing life to mean" throughout this book, so it should be clear that I am asserting that meaning does not exist until it is made and that life has no meaning until a meaning is forced upon it. Nothing could be emptier or sadder than to think endlessly about meaning but refrain from making any, to pine for meaning but not to work for it, to expect relief to arrive as you brood and worry.

Loving someone is action. Painting is action. Raising money for your documentary film is action. Thinking about your scientific theory is action. Playing catch with your daughter is action. Singing for 10,000 is action. Singing for one is action. Getting up from where you are sitting and going over to your writing pad and squeezing out five words is action. Not drinking when you are trying not to drink is action. Defending first principles is action. Making amends is action. Revising and submitting short stories from 20 years ago is action. Joining the Resistance is action. Creating is action.

We keep busy, but that is not the same as taking action. We know the difference between busyness and action by the way it feels in our body and by what it does for our heart. It may be that on a given day, making a pot of soup feels like the right action in support of our life plan, say because we are making it for friends out of a conscious effort to relate. On another day, making a pot of soup feels like busywork because we know that we are avoiding our creative work and squandering our time. Making a pot of soup, writing a short story, taking a day job, leaving a day job, anything that we do is right action only when it is right action.

To take the action that we want to take, we have to brave anxiety, opt to matter, and engage in the tasks I've been describing. To take even the simplest right action—writing a page of your screenplay, taking your saxophone out of moth balls, tackling the synopsis of your novel—often involves self-repair and transformation. To return to your saxophone after a decade of pining for music or to vacuum when vacuuming feels beneath your dignity are gigantic actions, heroic actions. An important action does not have to take you half-way around the world and may only cost you the expenditure of a few hundred calories, but it may also require incredible courage.

The Baroque composer and singer Barbara Strozzi, born in 1619, could not sing in public. Her culture would not allow it. What action did she take? Can you guess? Rather than abandoning music, she brought in her audience. She performed only in her own home and became one of the best-loved and best-known composers and singers of the Baroque era. Janet Nichols explained:

> Barbara Strozzi never performed anywhere but in her own home. She became an expert in writing chamber vocal works, music meant to be sung in a small room rather than a large opera house or concert hall. She composed over a hundred songs, including many for solo voice with keyboard or lute accompaniment. The large

number and the high quality of her compositions make her one of the most important composers of chamber vocal music of the Baroque era. She may be the only composer in all of history who earned wide acclaim without ever leaving her own home.

It is especially the act of creation that requires bravery. Our ability to make and maintain meaning is threatened by the intrinsic hardness of creative work. It is odd but true that most creators do not recognize this reality. Instead of crediting creating with being profoundly taxing, they chalk up their difficulties to personal weakness. This can't be their intention, any more than it would be the intention of a hiker who comes to the edge of a cliff to blame himself for not being able to fly. The hiker would say to himself, "How can I get down there? By rappelling? By going all the way around, even though it will take me a week?" Creators, faced by this cliff, say, "I am an idiot."

Creators blame themselves for the fact that it is hard to write a good novel or validate string theory. They come to the edge of their work and see the cliff, they find themselves in the middle of their work and experience the vertigo of not knowing, and instead of naming the cliff as the obstacle, they berate themselves. Why do they do this self-unfriendly thing? Because they know that they often do not try hard enough, so they generalize from this secret truth to the falsehood that it is all their fault, that their song or theory would materialize if only they had more guts, more discipline, a larger talent, more staying power.

What they need is more action and less berating. The hiker must do something or remain at the edge of that cliff until he starves to death. Creators must take action in service of their creative work. Rappelling may frighten them. Going around may take a year or a decade. Turning around and going home is no answer, as that is a path without heart. They must go forward, whether that means jumping off the cliff or taking the slow way around, composing a symphony in a hour, like Mozart, or composing a symphony in a decade, like Beethoven.

Melissa Padgett, an artist, teacher, and creativity coach, explained:

> *Action is a very healing, wonderful tonic. Whatever I do, succeed or fail, I usually feel more confident if I do something rather than sit around and wait. Some of my best coaching experiences have been when I suggest that the client do something right then. For instance, with my "never-enough-time" writing client I once said, "We have 10 minutes left. Would you be willing to spend it writing?" and we wrote some pieces in Natalie Goldberg's "keep the pen moving" style. The client had a visceral experience she loved and built on, and I went away thinking, "Finally! She did something!" That her writing was delightful was a cherry on top.*

Action is a wonderful tonic, as Melissa observed. Action heals. Maybe you are in a dead-end day job that is making you half-insane as you see your time slip away. Every day you work hard, but on few days do you take action in support of your life plan, your creativity, or your dreams. Of course you are depressed since the facts of existence disappoint you and you are not making much meaning. It will be only action that heals you: the action of taking a night class in Egyptian history, to give your brain something to chew on; the action of starting out every morning on your novel or making it to your studio every evening; the action of loving someone who, quite coincidentally, earns a living at work he or she enjoys, which allows you to quit your day job; the action of launching a new career; the action of sitting yourself down and determining if your day job can be made to feel more meaningful.

Vivian Brown, a painter and creativity coach, observed:

> *Aaagh! You mean reflecting and relating and believing I matter aren't enough? Planning and intending and making resolutions aren't*

enough? I've actually got to take steps, move forward, and do something? Turning thoughts into action is not my biggest talent. So I am going to write the following question in big letters and tape it above my desk: "What action will I engage in today in support of my creative life?" And when the day is done, I'll record the answers in a special journal of my accomplishments.

Our actions are our accomplishments. It is not satisfying to have a thought pop into our head and not write it down. It is not satisfying to dream of love but never to hold a lover's hand. What if you could do nothing to right wrongs? What if you found a pointed stick but never drew with it in the dirt? Could a brain kept alive by artificial means be anything less than permanently depressed? Unable to act, it might calculate pi to the thousandth place and still die of a broken heart.

Donna Lyons, a composer and creativity coach, reported:

> *Not so long ago, if I had been pressed to make a choice about the first thing I would recommend to a client who came to me for help, I doubt that I would have been able to choose among many reasonable possibilities. Now, having worked with more clients, I would say that if a creative person is having enough problems to seek help from a coach, he or she is by definition stuck, and the first option for consideration would be to get the rust-bound creative gears into some kind of motion, however creaky. Then, as the client comments on the experience of moving into action—or not moving into action—a coach can begin to determine which other areas needs attention.*

When you don't feel like acting, all hell breaks loose. Then you question your personality, the facts of existence, and the meaning of your life. You come home tired from work, you don't feel up to facing your nonfiction book, you start drinking, you sink. Your musical is stuck, it seems shallow and unmusical, you can't find the energy to revise it, you sink. When you say to yourself, "I can't," you are also saying, "Depression, come right in." You must teach yourself how to act when you don't feel like acting, when it is gloomy out, when chaos surrounds you, when your inner life is roiling madly, when you can't imagine acting.

It isn't that you must stay in a whir of motion. But you must learn to take the right action at the right split second. The split second when you are about to say, "I can't create today," is one of those split seconds. The split second when you hear yourself say, "I am a loser and the world sucks," is one of those split seconds. Take yourself by the shirt and pull yourself in the direction of action. Maybe you'll go kicking and screaming, maybe you'll experience vertigo and a panic attack, maybe you'll feel sick to your stomach. But you will thank yourself later.

PLANNING FOR ACTION

Plan to act. Have it in your mind that you are about to act. Have "I'm about to act" circulate in your brain so relentlessly that, just to quiet it, you act. Make simple plans: "I plan to write every day this week for two hours at least." Let go of the fear that you will fail yourself and not keep to your plan. Just keep reminding yourself, "I make plans, I break plans, I am never without a plan."

Rosemary Warden, writer and creativity coach, observed:

Planning, even just thinking about planning, has brought up fears for me in the past: fear of being forced to do something I haven't chosen myself, fear of failing to do the plan at all or less than effectively, and fear that the plan isn't the right plan.

These days, I approach a plan as something flexible and yielding, capable of being reviewed and revised. I give myself permission to change a plan when immersion in it suggests a new direction. Since planning can feel like "forcing" instead of "allowing creative juices to flow," I try to keep the "making myself do it" part reserved for getting myself to my desk. Once there, I let go into the freedom of the creative flow. Excitement takes over and the fears fade—mostly. I end up feeling happy that I've created a balance of "willing" and "allowing."

A drawback to planning for me is that it brings out my inner critic, which wants to judge whether I've lived up to the plan. When this judge appears, I often end up feeling depressed out of guilt for "not doing it well enough." Various writers advise ways to deal with the inner critic: Put it on the shelf, get angry at it and push it back, ignore it, etc. But what has worked best for me is to find ways to make it my ally: to dialog with it, update it on my current goals, and get it to agree to a less-harsh way of criticizing and evaluating.

The deepest fear about making plans is about taking action, period: that it won't be the "right" action. I've spent years not acting on what has the deepest meaning for me for fear that I might not make the right choice. What has helped me is to know that not taking action is like killing my creative self and to accept that being creative means making mistakes and messes. Affirming these things has helped me in my creative process and has also helped me feel more at ease in suggesting plans to clients and reassuring them that setting a plan doesn't mean setting themselves up for failure.

Now that I'm getting used to making plans for creative projects, I'm rather surprised that I'm beginning to see some of its positive aspects. I'm finding that making a plan for writing creates a better connection between me and the project, an alliance of sorts, that is firmer than if I just "think about" the project in a general way. Making a plan is like creating a vessel. The plan creates a place for the writing to be held and take a shape, the way a pottery jar holds grain. I still keep an eye on the plan so that it doesn't become too rigid a container. So in my analogy, the pottery jar is made of clay that never dries so that I can keep reshaping it as needed.

Your life is a campaign, a project. You are heroically forcing life to mean. You are the commanding general of your own army, ready to sacrifice weeks for the sake of a sculpture, ready to risk the pain of failed novels or dead-end theories. In the Introduction, I mentioned that, according to Arnold Ludwig's research, adventurers, militarists, and sports figures experience virtually no depression. They plan for action; they act; that is their life. Your job is the equivalent—to locate the headwaters of the Nile, to launch D-Day, to hit tape measure home runs—all translated into a sphere that matters to you.

LET US ACT

You come to see me in my capacity as a creativity coach. You say that you don't have any trouble singing in front of an audience of 10,000 but that singing in front of one other person makes you panic. There are many approaches I might take with you. We might discuss your history. I might teach you some performance anxiety strategies. But the approach that I am most likely to take is to ask you to sing for me, right here, right now. Of course, you won't want to get up and sing. Of course, you would much rather talk about the problem. My preference, however, is that you get up and try, that we enact the problem in real time. That way we get to see what is going on.

Maybe you come to see me and explain that you have the desire to paint more boldly. For some reason, boldness eludes you. Again, I will suggest that we act. I'll ask us to get up and stand in front of two imaginary blank canvases, you in front of yours and me in front of mine. "Let us paint!" I'll cry. I will make big, wild strokes in the air. You may not. Then we might talk about what seems to be going on, what seems to be holding your arm back. Then we'll try again. I'll paint boldly; maybe you will, too.

Maybe you come in to see me because you haven't been painting. We might have the following conversation:

"I haven't been painting," you say.

"Why don't you paint here?"

"Excuse me?"

"Why don't you paint right here? Maybe we can see what's going on."

"I can't."

"I'll go first." I stand up, face my invisible canvas, and start painting. "What am I feeling?"

"Stupid. Naked," you reply.

"Not excited? Full of ideas?"

"No. And that canvas in front of you—I can see by your gestures that it's much bigger than the ones I permit myself!"

"That's interesting. I'm having a darned good time. Care to join me?"

Maybe you come in to see me and say that you get to your writing every day but that distractions prevent you from writing for very long. I could inquire about that and ask questions: "What sort of distractions are we talking about? Internal ones? External ones?" We could investigate the phenomenon. But I am much more likely to say, "Why don't you write, and I'll distract you? Then we'll see what's going on." I'll give you a pad, wait for you to begin writing, and then clap loudly, or kick the table between us, or knock over my empty coffee cup. Maybe you'll laugh and not stop writing. Maybe you'll never stop again.

Maybe you come in to see me and say, "I'm having trouble taking risks with my art." I could broach the subject of anxiety or wonder about what sorts of risks you have in mind. But I'm more likely to lead us to the edge of my office rug, where we can make believe that we are standing at the edge of the Grand Canyon. There you can experience the vertigo and anxiety associated with leaping into a large creative project. Then I might send you to Arizona to repeat the exercise with the real thing.

Maybe you come in to see me and say, "I'm having trouble with my children's book. I can't seem to get the interaction right between the badger and the raccoon." What do you think I will do? I'm sure you can guess by now. I will ask you a few questions about the plot line and the characters and then I will say, "You be the badger, and I'll be the raccoon." We'll chat in character and let the book's problems fill the room.

Maybe you come in to see me and say, "I love acting, but I also want to direct. But I don't feel powerful enough to direct." We could talk about your childhood and identify the experiences that harmed you and sapped your courage. But I'm much more likely to say, "Why don't you direct me around the room? Send me from one place to another, tell me what you want me to do, tell me what you want me to say." In this way, you get to confront your fears, and I get to star in your first production.

I am happy to chat. But I am happier if we act.

WORTHY ACTION

The astounding painter Tamara de Lempicka—whose portraits of Count Furstenberg Herdringen, the Marquis d'Affitti, the Grand Duke Gabriel, and other notables of her acquaintance tell you everything you need to know about evil—painted brilliantly as a wild young woman. She prided herself on being an outsider ("I live on the fringe of society, and the rules of normal society have no currency for those on the fringe."), but she also craved riches, comfort, and a title. As the years passed, she moved further and further inside society, eventually marrying a baron and showing up at all the fashionable parties.

Gloria Vanderbilt remembers exclaiming to her mother as her mother prepared the guest list for a gala party, "Don't forget to invite Baroness Tamara de Lempicka-Kuffner. She is such fun, and her pictures are so amusing!" Tamara's daughter Kizette chronicled her mother's reaction when she heard of Gloria Vanderbilt's remark. Her mother shook her head and announced bitterly, "No artist worthy of the name could imagine a worse epitaph." Tamara de Lempicka's art and her life had traveled very far in the direction of ease, albeit always an uncomfortable ease, and from 1962 until her death in 1980 she never exhibited again. Her work had lost its power, and she was honest enough not to exhibit it.

If we don't consider our own actions worthy, we court depression. We must act, but we must act in accordance with our principles. We are constructing our own epitaph as we live, judging the actions we take and the actions we fail to take. We feel ill if we find ourselves merely amusing, merely adroit, merely clever. What we want from ourselves is to take one worthy action after another, resting only when we are exhausted, failing to uphold our ideals only occasionally, giving in only now and then to the shadows in our personality. Our neighbor across the street can do less, but that is his business.

Marcia Biasiello, a writer and creativity coach, observed:

If I don't do my creative work, the meaning in my life remains buried, and I get very lost. I worry endlessly about daily life and about life's biggest questions. I may look very busy and occupied, but my self is absent; it's somewhere else. Sometimes, the very act of creating something calms me down. It's like a focused exercise and fills in beautifully for meaningful work. Sometimes, the act of creating is the best I can do. It gets me into a place I need to be in order to get comfortable enough to fall into a deep work mode and really make some meaning. I may start out by feeling dull and un-

motivated, but taking action opens the door, and before long I am really working.

The door to meaning is closed but not locked. Taking action opens the door. Taking action turns hours into eternities. Make time count by taking some action that supports your life plan, your principles, and your creativity. Of course, you could ironically extol the virtues of inaction, of doing nothing, of lazing your way to death, of swinging in a hammock as you and the world spin pointlessly together. But that irony would only break your heart and get you nowhere.

15

MAKING MEANING

I've now described the tasks required of a creator if she hopes to make meaning, maintain meaning over time, and restore meaning when it drains away. Despite our discussion, you may not feel sanguine that you really understand what I mean by "making meaning." It's quite simple to say. You make meaning by striving to live your personal vision of the good, which, as a creative person, includes creating. You make meaning by being a righteous human being who minimizes the worst in her and uses her freedom to be her best self.

When you make meaning, you are guided by an internal dialogue centered around one question: "What is the righteous thing to do?" Is it righteous to accept that I am unable to create because the harm done to me as a child has made me weak and afraid? Or it is more righteous to create, even though I feel ruined? Is it righteous to be writing this novel? Or should I be writing that one? Is it righteous to succumb to meaning substitutes? Or should I clean up my act? Making meaning is simply doing good on this earth, while you can, according to your own lights, and despite everything.

HEROIC MEANING-MAKING

Will it feel good to translate books from one language into another, so as to eke out a living, and then paint small miniatures in the evening, miniatures that no one will buy? Will it feel good to study a corner of mathematics that has no practical application and that, if it ever did, might only be used by make new weapons? Will it feel good to act in commercials for tennis shoes and bathroom deodorants when you want to perform in great plays, move people to tears, and make a name for yourself as an artist? How can you call your life righteous in the circumstances you find yourself, so far from where you want to be?

By remembering that you are not a cosmic joke, that the cosmos has no sense of humor, and that if your reality seems ridiculous to you, you must change it. You do this by taking a single step in a desired direction, then a second step, then a third step. The first step might be creating your life plan sentence; the second step might be committing to it; the third step might be taking some action in support of your plan. The first step might be finally writing your novel; the second step might be painstakingly revising it; the third step might be revising it again. The first step might be opening up to love; the second step might be opening up a little more; the third step might be opening up still more.

You may be thinking, "How lovely to hear 'Just change it!' As if I can suddenly change from being a frustrated nobody to a successful creator who lives a righteous life and is masterful at keeping meaning afloat! How, all of a sudden, can I squeeze a nice living out of writing poetry? How can I make my day job less taxing and demeaning? How can I silence the demons in my own brain? How can I find love when I feel quite unlovable? How can I be Mozart when I feel less than Salieri? How can I act righteously when I am so irritable, so disappointed, so beleaguered? How can I get somewhere that I can't even envision? Hearing 'Just change it!' is the essence of cold comfort."

Nevertheless, that is my message.

Your job is to live in a way that makes you feel proud of yourself, to live that way today, tomorrow, and every day thereafter. If that means creating flower paintings, researching the Crusades, launching guerrilla theater, or playing ancient music from your native land, that is what you will do. If you can truthfully say, "I am proud of the work I am trying to do," and, "I am proud of the person I am trying to be," you are on the right path. If you can't, you must change.

Maybe you agree with me wholeheartedly. The question still in your mind is, "How can I possibly maintain my intention?" You have a studio full of the canvases you've painted. Few are as powerful as you wish they would be. You think about starting a new canvas, and you hear yourself say, "I can't. It doesn't make any sense to paint. Painting doesn't matter." How can you find the will to continue? Only by virtue of your practiced response to this meaning crisis, a response you have learned to employ the instant you court meaninglessness.

It might be a loud, "No! I am going to paint!" It might be a gentle conversation with yourself, in which you remind yourself about your love of color and your love of the experience of losing yourself in your work. It might be the way you have learned to breathe through the moment, the way you have learned not to take your objections seriously, the way you have learned that you are only experiencing anxiety. But it must be something. You must possess practiced responses to these meaning threats and meaning crises, or else paralysis and depression will set in.

If you don't possess this practiced response, you will opt for a meaning substitute like a drunken brawl, a pound of chocolate, an action drama on television. Without practiced responses to deal with the pain of reality and the meaning crises that come, one after another, your intention will crumble under the weight of too much defeat. This is your heroic work. You choose yourself and then you keep choosing yourself, again and again, as long as you live.

In *Art and Artist*, Otto Rank argued that creators are individuals who "nominate themselves." In Rank's view, the entire explanation for the birth of a novel, symphony, painting, or scientific theory is that a human being has nominated himself as a real worker in that field, has said "I can do this," and ignores all cultural, social, religious, and even psychological injunctions against becoming a fervent, even a fanatical, creator. Poverty is simply a terrible inconvenience. Failures are simply nasty facts of existence. Marketplace and institutional realities are simply facts to be braved and challenges to be met. This hero is you, if only you will nominate yourself.

Perhaps you have a beautiful voice, but performing makes you feel very anxious. Should you make meaning in a way other than singing, or should you strive to manage your performance anxiety? Only you can say. Perhaps you've written a novel but can't find a publisher. Should you make meaning with a new novel, make meaning in a way other than writing fiction, redouble your efforts to sell your novel, or what? Only you can say. This is the heroism required of you: to reckon with the facts of your existence, to make hard choices, and to keep meaning afloat even as you struggle.

Even those of you who agree with the picture I've been painting, who believe that meaning is the issue, and who would like to become personal meaning masters, must still be troubled by the place I am leaving you: alone, needing to figure out how you will force life to mean. What are you supposed to do in the next few seconds? Later today? Tomorrow morning? What are you supposed to do when you find yourself procrastinating and not painting? What are you supposed to do when your novel remains unpublished? What are you supposed to do when you achieve a success that nevertheless does not answer your meaning questions? What technique or strategy will you employ when your day job bores you, drains you of energy, and puts your creative life on hold? The answer to every question of this sort is, "What you figure out to do." That is the heroism required of you. That is what making meaning means.

FOR THE SAKE OF A PEACH

Picasso once remarked that if he painted a still life for the sake of a single peach, viewers would see the peach only as a detail and not as the painting's central reason for being. Of course, viewers reacted that way because the painting did not point an arrow at the peach, as an advertisement for peaches might, but incorporated the peach in a seamless totality, a carefully constructed gestalt. In fact, Picasso had lavished equal attention on the peach and on the painting as a whole, even if in his heart the peach mattered the most.

The same might be true for your life. On a given day, you may live for the sake of one certain hour, the hour when you perform your songs in a nightclub or write your novel. In a sense, you live your whole day for the sake of that peach, that detail, that hour. But you also contrive to turn your day into a seamless gestalt, a total creation, during which you make meaning second-by-second and hour-by-hour as you actively live the many and varied elements of your life plan. The hour or two or three that you do your creative work may mean the most to you, but the rest of your day is not a void, a blank, an incipient meaning crisis.

One hour you have coffee with a lover or a friend. That is its own brand of meaning. For several hours you do work for others, work made less painful by your authenticity, your creativity, your high ideals, your righteousness. Your way of being makes those hours, if not meaningful, at least something other than a meaning drain or meaning crisis. For a half-hour you sit in the sun, watch people pass by, and enjoy the simple meaning of life moving around you. For an hour or two you indulge in some meaning substitute, living a fairy tale romance with a novel or beating the bad guys with an action movie, easy with this innocent meaning substitute because you know you are sandwiching it between periods of meaning-making.

Not every minute of this long day is perfect. Not every minute is painless. Not every minute is as meaningful as the time you spend creating. Still, meaning is maintained throughout the day. You may be living for the peach, but the whole painting is admirable and even beautiful. If you feel in your heart that you are following your principles and not living carelessly, if you feel that the gestalt of this day makes sense even though parts of it are not to your liking, then this will be a day without a meaning crisis and without a depression.

You try to perfect your life, without imagining for a moment that you can. You try to increase the amount of time you spend on your creative efforts, knowing that on some days it will be very hard to create. You try to increase the amount of love in your life, the amount you get and the amount you give. You monitor what you are doing and put yourself in charge of maintaining meaning. On some days, because the universe is neither benign nor malicious, you feel happy. On rarer days, a miracle of the following sort occurs.

Franz Liszt wrote of his childhood visit to Beethoven:

> I was about eleven years old when my respected teacher Czerny took me to see Beethoven. Beethoven had such an aversion to infant prodigies that he persistently refused to see me, but at last Czerny, indefatigable, persuaded him. Beethoven was sitting at a long, narrow table near the window, working. For a time he scrutinized us grimly and remained silent when my good teacher called me to the piano. When I finished my first piece, Beethoven asked me whether I could play a fugue by Bach. I did so; then he said, "Could you also transpose this fugue into another key?" Fortunately, I could.
>
> After the final chord, I looked up. The Master's darkly glowing gaze was fixed upon me penetratingly. Yet suddenly a benevolent smile broke up his gloomy features. Beethoven came quite close, bent over me, laid his hand on my head, and repeatedly stroked my hair. I plucked up courage and asked, "May I play something of yours now?" He nodded with a smile and I played the first movement of the C major Concerto. When I had ended, Beethoven seized my

*hands, kissed me on the forehead, and said gently: "Off with you!
You're a happy fellow, for you'll give happiness and joy to many
other people. There is nothing better or greater than that!"*

*This event in my life remained my greatest pride, the palladium
for my whole artistic career. I speak of it only very rarely and only
to my intimate friends.*

A small miracle occurred in the life of Beethoven and the life of
Liszt. In a sea of depression, Beethoven received a gift of connection
and a moment of happiness. He received it, however, only because he
forced himself to do what was anathema to him, suffering another
music teacher and his prodigy. Why did Beethoven allow the young
Liszt to visit? Because Czerny was so persuasive? As if even the most
persuasive music teacher could have budged Beethoven! He allowed
Liszt to visit because, in fierce debate with himself, he opted for hope
rather than hopelessness. To refuse an audience to all prodigies would
have been to curse the future, to hate life with a vengeance, even to
reject music. On this day, he sided with hope.

UNDERSTANDING AND
MANAGING YOUR DEPRESSION

A person who breaks free of the need to parrot the beliefs of others
and who nominates herself as her own final arbiter of meaning will,
as she confronts the facts of existence, find existence wanting and will
find her ability to make and maintain meaning sorely taxed. The anxiety and sadness she experiences as a result of finding existence
wanting and meaning endangered will precipitate a depression, existential in nature and not psychological, biological, or social.

In order to deal with existence as she finds it and in order to
make sufficient meaning, a creator faces difficult tasks which, by

virtue of their real difficulty, require true heroism on her part. She must brave anxiety. She must rebuild her personality and choose worthy creative projects. She must bear up under the pain of not creating well enough or often enough and the pain of losing vast amounts of time to work done to pay the bills. She must do the things I have outlined in this book: They are many, and they are hard.

Søren Kierkegaard wrote:

> One sticks one's finger into the soil to tell by its smell in what land one is in. I stick my finger into existence—it smells of nothing. Where am I? Who am I? How came I here? What is this thing called the world? Who lured me into this thing and now leaves me here? Why was I not consulted, why was I just thrust into its ranks? How did I obtain an interest in this big enterprise they call reality? Why should I have an interest in it? And if I am compelled to take part in it, where is the director?

We have come to a time in our history when it is no longer useful to ask about the whereabouts of the director or to pine about his absence. We must force life to mean even though we are bereft of the instruction manual we crave, the guidance we desire, the answers we feel we need. Those questions no longer serve us because their answers are shrouded in complete mystery. We live knowing only that we can choose to live properly, as befits what is best in our nature, creating symphonies, holding another person's hand, rising to uphold a principle. On some dark nights, when the pain of existence and cosmic meaninglessness tear at our soul, we will find ourselves crying bitter tears. Then we dry our eyes and begin again.

Two thousand years ago, the Roman Epictetus admonished:

> Now is the time to get serious about living your ideals. How long can you afford to put off being who you really want to be? Put your principles into practice—now. This is your life! You aren't a child anymore. The longer you wait, the more you will be vulnerable

to mediocrity and filled with shame and regret, because you know
you are capable of better. From this instant on, vow to stop disap-
pointing yourself. Separate yourself from the mob. Decide to be ex-
traordinary and do what you need to do—now.

The picture I am painting may not be accurate. While I doubt it, depression may have nothing to do with meaning, nothing to do with the facts of existence, nothing to do with freedom, responsibility, and the other ideas existentialists promote. I am asking so very much of you that it will be a stroke of real luck, a true blessing, if, for instance, your depression can be completely treated pharmaceutically. I understand that part of you would like your depression to be something other than existential.

Perhaps it is, in whole or in part. Perhaps antidepressants can provide you with the complete answer. Perhaps psychotherapy can help you unravel a personality knot or air a childhood trauma and thereby provide a cure. Perhaps a sun lamp, more exercise, and a different diet will positively affect your mood. But when we look at the forces at play in the psyche of creators, when we look at what they dream of doing and the demons of meaninglessness with which they wrestle, it is foolhardy to ignore what we can plainly see.

What do you think? I return these matters to your examination. This is no intellectual puzzle to be solved but your life to live. In an introduction to existentialism, Nathan Scott explained, "The real bite of existence is to be felt in the deep things of personal experience which make us know—through love and sorrow, through nostalgia and joy, through death and loss—that a human life is not an intellectual puzzle to be ferreted out but a gift to be received and a task to be fulfilled." You may be of two minds as to whether your life is a gift, but I hope you have no doubt that it is a task to be fulfilled.

When we are not true to ourselves, we suffer. When we are true to ourselves, we suffer. This is not a cosmic joke, just a consequence of the facts of existence as they are. So we say, "I will do my creative work, even though I may suffer." We say, "I won't try to ward off pain by not creating, as that only brings its own, worse brand of suffering." We say, "Authenticity rubs me right up against suffering, but it is the only way I can take pride in myself." Camus wrote, "If there is a soul, it is a mistake to believe that it is given to us fully created. Rather it is created here, throughout a whole life. And living is nothing else but that long and painful bringing forth."

Perhaps making meaning is just an illusion, a trick you play on yourself in order to go on. What if it is? As Sheila Ballantyne put it, "Some of my best friends are illusions." In the end, we have to laugh at our worries and our razor-edged ability to doubt. We must simply choose belief, not in gods or in a compassionate universe but in the necessity that we honor our life-until-death. To live carelessly, not choosing to matter, and fearfully, derailed by stray worries and self-attacks, is to beg for depression. Better to make a best friend out of the illusion that there is meaning to be made.

I invited several people to read *The Van Gogh Blues* in manuscript. One of them, Mickey Birnbaum, playwright and screenwriter, sent me the following response. His story is an excellent summary of the territory we have traveled in this book. Mickey wrote:

> I've been a screenwriter for seventeen years now. It's hard to imagine a business that pays so well (when it pays) yet treats artists so poorly. Over the course of the first ten years of my career, I took studio assignments, largely for movies in which things blow up and people shoot guns. After ten years, I soured on this experience. A lot of the time, I was asked to rewrite scripts in ways I knew were technically or thematically wrong—in effect, I was being required to do bad work. Meanwhile, I was really hungry to LEARN and grow as a writer, and frustrated that, even though I was making money, I hadn't had a movie made.
>
> So I sat down and wrote a script, straight from the heart. Al-

though the first draft was mediocre, it came to the attention of a small company which shepherded me through subsequent drafts, and then sold the script to a Hollywood studio. Finally, the movie was made, and it was a great experience. The director kept me involved in the creative process throughout filming (this doesn't happen often—usually writers are removed from their own project and replaced with other writers). I even got to be on set to observe filming. It was a fabulous learning experience, even though the final product was inferior to what it could or should have been.

It was satisfying to have a movie released, to realize a goal eleven years in the making. But I had a big realization after the film's release. Successes, as well as failures, come and go. Pretty much everything's transient. I had worked hard to achieve this goal (as it happened, the film was unsuccessful, and so did nothing to advance my career), it had arrived, it had gone, and now . . . what? I guess you'd say this was a major shattering of my meaning-vessel. Despite intellectually "knowing better," I had nourished the illusion that getting a movie made would somehow justify or enlighten me. It didn't. Still, I knew I wanted to continue to develop my own voice, and I made a commitment to writing scripts that I believed in.

Somewhat humbled, determined to become a better writer and continue to make money at my craft, I proceeded. Two scripts followed. The first sold quickly and paid well. I had a great time rewriting the script for the producers and studio who bought it. But ultimately, the film never got made. The next script came to me in one of those rare bursts of inspiration that come only a few times in a writer's life (if he's lucky). As I wrote it, I wondered if it would make sense to anyone, or just seem outrageous and baffling. But I needed to write it. I recognized, for the first time, my VOICE. People had a warm reaction to the script, but because the material was challenging, by Hollywood standards, it took a year to sell it. After one rewrite, the producers and studio removed me from my own project and replaced me with other writers. They had lied to me and assured me that they would keep me on-board as the writer. Eventually, as with so many other scripts, the studio lost interest and shelved the project.

This was the beginning of a long period of depression which extended from 1999 almost to now. I felt betrayed, hurt, vulnerable. I felt my heroic efforts to do true and meaningful work as a screenwriter were pointless, as my work would only be mutilated and/or shelved. I felt completely isolated from the things I loved about movies—the ability to transport viewers to another world, or the ability to allow people to recognize themselves in a story. I wanted to make movies, but I had ended up spending fifteen years spinning my wheels. I wasn't sure I was willing to spend another fifteen years doing the same. Plus, my hunger for learning was greater than ever. I wanted, more than anything, even through this depression, to become a better writer. It was the only vessel of meaning that still held for me, the only thing that looked remotely like a PATH.

I considered other career choices, but none appealed to me. Despite the pain and confusion of depression, I decided two things: I would write another screenplay, and at the same time, I would find a complementary way to pursue my art that would be free of financial considerations, and would enable me to LEARN. Eventually, this decision led me back to theatre. I started to write plays as well as screenplays, and hooked up with a local philanthropic arts organization that sponsors workshops and labs for playwrights. This year, my first play was chosen by the same organization to receive a staged reading as part of an annual New Works Festival attended by artistic directors from around the country. For the past three years, I've been part of a playwrights' group that has given me a sense of creative community completely absent in Hollywood. And, boy, have I been learning. A lot of it goes into my playwriting, but I bring it back to my screenplays too, and I think they are better for it.

I took an incredibly long and circuitous route to arrive at a

place where I could embrace the art that really nourishes me. I'm
not sure yet why my path has been so long, why I've been in denial,
but this feels like an important question. Second, my meaning-
vessel, so often broken and replaced, has been getting bigger, more
inclusive, since I made this decision. At the same time, I'm shifting
from identifying myself as a screenwriter/playwright to a play-
wright/screenwriter. Third, I'm still depressed! The film script I
wrote from the heart has renewed interest from a new studio, a big
star, and a name director. The script I wrote after that—another
iconoclastic script in my own voice—was received even more en-
thusiastically than the last one (although it's been difficult to sell
as well). My play reading established me as a part of a theatrical
community I love, and opened doors for me. My wife and I just cel-
ebrated our tenth wedding anniversary. Still, even as I move forward, as I take action and do my best to summon my courage, my
meaning crisis continues.

I am shaping meaning as I go, though not until I read The Van
Gogh Blues could I articulate what I was doing. Even now, if you
asked me what "means" for me, I'd have trouble saying. The idea of
bearing witness comes to mind, of saying no to power, of making
people laugh, of relieving suffering. I had one flash, though, after
reading The Van Gogh Blues. I do have a spiritual sense of the
world (though that has yet to be fully articulated), and it strikes
me that humans are here precisely to make meaning, that without
our meaning-making there would be no meaning, only a sterile, un-
perceived machine-universe. And without ambivalence there can be
no meaning—without doubt, without mistakes, without confusion, without striving, there is only singular, uninflected, unin-
spired flatness. So maybe creating meaning is an end—a holy
end—in itself.

CONCLUSION

I have presented an existential view of depression and the creative person. I have argued that the depression creative people experience is fundamentally caused by their upsetness with the facts of existence and their difficulties in making and maintaining meaning. In doing this, I have intentionally minimized the role of biology in depression. However, I have also repeatedly pointed out that, even if I am right in my views, it is still imperative that creators investigate medical treatment for their depression since biological remedies have been proven to reduce the experience of depression in thousands upon thousands of sufferers—even if the antidepressants employed do nothing to solve a creator's existential problems.

Just as I have minimized the role of biology in depression, I have also minimized the role of psychology and "mental illness." I have done this for several reasons, all of which I have mentioned already: that "mental illness" requires quotes since no one knows what it is and since every practitioner means something different by it, that psychological theories are more literary than scientific and do not stand up to even mild scrutiny, and that attaching labels to bundles of symptoms and calling a person "bipolar" or "borderline" is not the same as understanding what is going on. Despite these objections, it is nevertheless obvious that psychological motives are at play in our lives, that psychological problems constellate in characteristic ways, and that a wise and supportive psychotherapist can make a positive difference in your life.

Biological treatment is likely to help, and psychotherapeutic treatment may possibly help. Other remedies are also available and should not be scorned. A lack of sunshine precipitates depression in many people, and the use of a light box is a simple solution that may bring real relief. Changing diet can help, as can regular exercise. Whole books address the various aspects of this larger picture: depression associated with menopause, depression associated with winter, depression associated with giving birth, depression associated with chronic illness, depression associated with major life changes like divorce.

The picture I have painted is not complete. But it is accurate. If you get a nasty rejection letter in the mail and the enterprise of writing suddenly seems meaningless to you, you will get depressed. The depression arises not just because your ego has been bruised, which would be a psychological cause, but because you are reminded of essential meaninglessness, that dark specter hovering above every contemporary creative person's shoulder. When this meaning crisis strikes, you must immediately confront the fact that meaning has taken a blow. You don't have a moment to lose. If you rush to the Scotch bottle, if you fall down and grieve, if you deny your pain and try to put on a happy face, you are begging for depression. What you must say to yourself is, "Meaning crisis." Then you must do what you have learned to do to restore meaning.

The headline I want you to take away is that you must restore meaning immediately after each blow to meaning, just as you must stop the bleeding when an artery is severed. You can't ignore meaning crises any more than you can ignore other catastrophes. You were not taught at home or in school to deal with meaning, to think about meaning, or to make meaning, but you can't use your lack of training as an excuse. The stakes are too high. If you can't keep meaning afloat, you will sink.

How you actually accomplish this work is your learning of a lifetime. Part of the answer is the basic attitude you adopt, the basic heroism you show moment-in and moment-out. Part of the answer is understanding and managing your self-talk and getting a grip on your own mind. Part of the answer is doing worthy creative work, work that pleases you, makes you proud, and inoculates you against meaning losses. Part of the answer is repairing yourself, rebuilding your brain, your body, and your personality in your own best image. These are the core tasks we have been discussing throughout this book.

You may be a great painter, writer, composer, or scientist. But if you haven't learned how to effectively deal with meaning crises, you will get depressed. Your next hundred paintings will not be enough to save you: look at van Gogh. Your next Ninth Symphony will not be enough to save you: look at Beethoven. Your next *War and Peace* will not be enough to save you: look at Tolstoy. What will save you is your expert work at forcing life to mean. You are free to choose your meanings since meaning is entirely up for grabs. But you are also obliged to choose your meanings, as meaning means nothing until you tell the universe where you stand.

APPENDIX:
YOUR VOCABULARY
OF MEANING

As you work to make and maintain meaning, it will help if you build a vocabulary of words and phrases that allow you to converse about meaning. Then you can discuss with yourself how some meaning events, like meaning drains and meaning losses, precipitate depression, while other meaning events, like meaning investments and meaning opportunities, prevent depression. If you build a working vocabulary of meaning, you will have significantly bettered your chances of managing your existential situation.

Build your vocabulary of meaning with words and phrases that strike you as meaningful. You may prefer psychological language, spiritual language, existential language, or philosophical language. No words work for everyone, not even the word "meaning." All words are complex bundles of meanings, and a word that has a positive resonance for one person may have a negative resonance for someone else, or no resonance at all. Put words and phrases on the table as possible candidates for inclusion in your vocabulary of meaning and examine each one to see whether it actually holds some meaning for you.

Think of words like ego, archetype, soul, passion, freedom, responsibility. Any of these words might appear in your personal vocabulary of meaning. By the same token, none might find a place. In mine, you would find the words action, absurdity, ambiguity, choice, commitment, complexity, courage, doubt, engagement, intention, mystery, risk, and uncertainty. What words and phrases will your vocabulary of meaning contain?

Following are 60 phrases, some of which you may find useful to include in your vocabulary of meaning. Try them out in conversation with yourself. Imagine planning a fine "meaning adventure," or discuss with yourself what you will do when a "meaning crisis" strikes. Consider what might cause a "meaning leak" or what constitutes a "meaning opportunity." Enjoy these phrases, think about them, and incorporate them into your vocabulary of meaning if they feel useful.

Rather than define these 60 terms, which would make for too long an Appendix, I'll present a single possible usage for each one. I think you'll get the gist of the phrase from the way it's employed.

60 TERMS FOR A VOCABULARY OF MEANING

1. Meaning Accident
Possible usage: "That editor inviting me to write a book about islands was a meaning accident that affected how I've made meaning for the past two years."

2. Meaning Adventure
Possible usage: "When I started writing my novel about the lives of expatriate Americans in India, it felt like the beginning of a great meaning adventure."

3. Meaning Analysis

Possible usage: "Because the task provokes anxiety, few people engage in conscious meaning analysis."

4. Meaning Boost

Possible usage: "My first three novels failed to sell. When a publisher bought my fourth novel, that was an amazing meaning boost that allowed me to devote my life to fiction."

5. Meaning Conflict

Possible usage: "Every time I start a painting, I find myself embroiled in a meaning conflict, torn between believing that painting is meaningful and believing that painting is ridiculous."

6. Meaning Constellation

Possible usage: "World War II and everything that it stands for is a meaning constellation for me. I enjoy World War II books and movies and love to sculpt images that relate to that time."

7. Meaning Container

Possible usage: "I hope that I'm doing the right thing by pouring meaning into acting. For now, acting feels like a meaning container capable of holding my beliefs and dreams."

8. Meaning Crisis

Possible usage: "My usual way is to get enthusiastic about some project, then get down on myself, then experience a meaning crisis. After a few weeks, I feel a little renewed enthusiasm, and the cycle starts all over."

9. Meaning Disruption

Possible usage: "I woke up this morning with the plot for my screenplay almost clear in my mind. But the roof started leaking, which made for a serious meaning disruption."

10. Meaning Disturbance

Possible usage: "I was writing my novel and suddenly experienced a meaning disturbance when I heard myself say, 'This novel is stupid, and I'm an idiot for wasting my time on it.'"

11. Meaning Divestment

Possible usage: "I've decided to become a part-time freelance writer. Therefore, I'm making a meaning divestment from my career of the last 10 years, career counseling. I don't want career counseling to lose all of its meaning, but I need to make meaning investments elsewhere."

12. Meaning Drain

Possible usage: "I find my brother a real meaning drain. Every time I see him, he wonders why I refuse to get a normal career, why I think I have a chance of competing—and succeeding—against 10,000 other actors, and what makes me think I'm so special."

13. Meaning Effort

Possible usage: "It's going to take quite a meaning effort to make my administrative job feel meaningful, but I'm going to make that meaning effort because I'm not ready to quit."

14. Meaning Enthusiasm

Possible usage: "I've always loved music and wanted to make my life in it. But that love seemed to translate into nothing more than one mere meaning enthusiasm after another. So I have no more faith in meaning enthusiasms; or maybe I have no more faith in myself."

15. Meaning Environment

Possible usage: "I thought this university would prove to be a solid meaning environment. But I've discovered how little thoughtful work gets done here and how petty rivalries define the place. So I'm thinking about moving to London, which must be a thriving meaning environment."

16. Meaning Ethics

Possible usage: "Meaning ethics is the study of the relationship between meaning and ethics, a wonderful 21st-century field waiting to be explored."

17. Meaning Event

Possible usage: "I had a profound meaning event this morning when I realized that I do not need to know who my birth parents are and that I can stop looking for them and pining for them."

18. Meaning Field

Possible usage: "Since I've become an investigative reporter, corruption in politics is the meaning field in which I operate."

19. Meaning Focus

Possible usage: "I can't seem to keep my intention to aggressively market my paintings in meaning focus. Maybe selling makes me anxious, or maybe it holds no meaning for me."

20. Meaning Fog

Possible usage: "I've been in a meaning fog ever since I abandoned the novel I was writing."

21. Meaning Frustration

Possible usage: "I experience mild meaning frustration as I wait to hear from literary agents about my book proposal and serious meaning frustration when a rejection letter arrives."

22. Meaning Impermanence

Possible usage: "This has been a time of meaning impermanence for me as I wrestle with the idea of leaving my day job and worry that I won't be able to find anything worth a new meaning investment."

23. Meaning Intention

Possible usage: "My meaning intention with respect to my novel has been strong all month. I go to the computer first thing each morning and stay put for at least three hours."

24. Meaning Investment

Possible usage: "I'm about to make a big meaning investment in the idea that psychological research can be meaningful by choosing to get a doctorate in social psychology."

25. Meaning Invitation

Possible usage: "My creativity coach offered me a welcome meaning invitation when she wondered if I wanted to return to the book of essays I've put aside for six months."

26. Meaning Lapse

Possible usage: "I was fully committed to this suite of abstract paintings, and then one day I heard myself say, 'Only realistic paintings matter.' That meaning lapse caused me to stop painting for a week, but then I recommitted to abstraction and made a meaning reinvestment."

27. Meaning Leak

Possible usage: "The rejection letter that arrived yesterday produced a serious meaning leak and made me want to abandon writing. But I licked my wounds and made an immediate meaning reinvestment in the enterprise of writing."

28. Meaning Loss

Possible usage: "I experience meaning losses with such terrible regularity that I am always on the verge of a meaning crisis or else in the middle of one."

29. Meaning Metaphor

Possible usage: "Sculpting is a powerful meaning metaphor for me. I love to sculpt, but I also love the constellation of meaning that sculpture represents."

30. Meaning Misadventure

Possible usage: "I now think that working in plastic was a meaning misadventure. I learned a lot, but I also abandoned my true love, stone."

31. Meaning Mistake

Possible usage: "Although I understand why I did it, spending so much time copying the old masters was a meaning mistake that prevented me from finding out where I needed to make my own meaning investments."

32. Meaning Mode
Possible usage: "The last time I was in a meaning mode was last Wednesday when I worked on my symphony."

33. Meaning Moment
Possible usage: "Accepting my first painting commission was a significant meaning moment for me. I realized that I was for hire, which radically altered my self-image."

34. Meaning Movement
Possible usage: "This morning I thought my new novel would be set in Burma. By evening, I knew that it had to be set in a London suburb. There's been such tremendous meaning movement today that I feel like I've traveled halfway around the world."

35. Meaning Opportunity
Possible usage: "Spending a year studying traditional Irish music will prove a rich meaning opportunity."

36. Meaning Orientation
Possible usage: "Given my meaning orientation, I'd rather admit to ignorance than posit gods in whom I don't believe."

37. Meaning Pattern
Possible usage: "I am sensing a rich meaning pattern emerging in the stage play I'm writing."

38. Meaning Permanence
Possible usage: "Is meaning permanence even desirable if it rests on the belief that one's sect has all the answers?"

39. Meaning Potential
Possible usage: "Many art disciplines hold meaning potential for me, but making a meaning investment in any one of them would just keep me in poverty."

40. Meaning Problem
Possible usage: "I find physics intellectually interesting, but no amount of scientific knowledge can solve the meaning problems in my life."

41. Meaning Reinvestment

Possible usage: "I'm experiencing burnout, teaching the same chemistry classes year in and year out. But the subject matter of chemistry hasn't lost its meaning for me. I want to make a meaning reinvestment in chemistry by embarking on some new research."

42. Meaning Respite

Possible usage: "Between finishing my last novel and starting on my next novel, I'm taking a meaning respite. I'm going to eat a little too much chocolate, watch some romantic movies, and not worry about meaning."

43. Meaning Restoration

Possible usage: "While in Florence, I experienced a meaning restoration that will help me work hard on my book about frescoes."

44. Meaning Risk

Possible usage: "It's a meaning risk to suppose that sociology is the right place to make a major meaning investment. But I have to declare my major, and I'm inclined to look at choosing sociology as a meaning opportunity."

45. Meaning Shift

Possible usage: "I experienced a meaning shift when I visited Iceland and learned that a high literacy rate and a high illegitimacy rate can coexist beautifully."

46. Meaning Spark

Possible usage: "The French movie I saw today was a meaning spark that caused me to rush home and resume work on my stage play."

47. Meaning Stability

Possible usage: "I experienced a long period of meaning stability, but at a high cost. During that period, I would only make paintings that I thought customers would want."

48. Meaning Strain

Possible usage: "I've been struggling so hard to figure out what I want to compose next that I've pulled a muscle in my brain and given myself a meaning strain."

49. Meaning Substitute

Possible usage: "I couldn't get to work on my novel, so I settled for some meaning substitutes instead, first by reading the newspaper, then by reading a novel, then by watching an action movie."

50. Meaning Sum

Possible usage: "Today's meaning sum was miserably small, and if I don't make some concerted meaning efforts tomorrow, I am going to get in a real funk."

51. Meaning Support

Possible usage: "The art books in my library are meaning supports for me. Their presence reminds me that I am not alone in opting to make meaning via painting."

52. Meaning Surge

Possible usage: "I visited the art museum today and experienced a palpable meaning surge. All at once, my desire to sculpt was violently reawakened."

53. Meaning Surrender

Possible usage: "The meaning surrender I made last week, when I stopped composing, felt like an act of cowardice. But somehow it allowed me to relax a little, and now I feel prepared to make a meaning reinvestment in my music."

54. Meaning Task

Possible usage: "I've set myself the meaning task of better understanding evolution."

55. Meaning Tension

Possible usage: "I've been under a lot of meaning tension recently as I try to decide whether I should continue to make meaning as a new genre public artist."

56. Meaning Thread

Possible usage: "I have a few novels in mind to write, but the one I'm tackling is about a man who tries to opt out of society. Whether it's possible to opt out of society is a meaning thread I haven't yet explored in my work."

57. Meaning Threat

Possible usage: "I'm excited to be meeting with literary agents at this upcoming writers' conference, but I'm also experiencing it as a meaning threat. Anything negative they say could affect my self-image and precipitate a meaning crisis."

58. Meaning Vacuum

Possible usage: "As soon as I stop writing, I feel at such a loss that all I can think of doing is going to bed. The meaning vacuum I enter each time I stop writing is an amazingly dynamic, empty place."

59. Meaning Web

Possible usage: "I've finally identified some of the meaning threads tangled up in my meaning web. When I decide which thread interests me the most, that's the direction I'll take my art."

60. Meaning Wound

Possible usage: "When I realized that my novel would never be published, I experienced a meaning wound so painful that I thought I would die. The wound hasn't healed yet, though it's been 10 years since I put that manuscript away."

Emma Muhlberger, an artist and graphic designer, was an early reader of this book. She described her reaction to my ideas in the following way:

> I had been sniffing around the issue of meaning in relation to my life after doing some years of intensive work on my own suppressed creative self. I hadn't actually linked my past depression with

my search for meaning, although I noticed that once I started creating, the depression only encroached for a day or two at a time, not for whole months. But I still had trouble articulating what the problem was when I felt depressed. I could feel the numbness, but the best I could come up with was, "Something's not right." Of course, that meant that I had no direction to take to deal with the problem. Your book, and especially encountering your new lexicon of meaning, has changed everything. Phrases like 'meaning crisis" and "meaning leak" fit perfectly for me. I now feel a little bit magical because, as the phrase has it, "you have power over that which can be named." Now I know what to say and how to think when my mind wanders into the world of "why bother, it doesn't matter anyway."

I hope these 60 terms give you a head start on building your own vocabulary of meaning. As with everything I've presented in this book, I welcome your thoughts and comments. You can contact me using the contact information provided on page 257. Thanks, and good luck!

ENDNOTES

INTRODUCTION

p. 4   *The Price of Greatness: Resolving the Creativity and Madness Controversy.* Arnold Ludwig. New York City: Guilford Publications, 1995.

p. 9   In *Existential Psychotherapy.* Irvin D. Yalom. New York City: Basic Books, 1980.

In *Touched with Fire: Manic-Depressive Illness and the Artistic Temperament.* Kay Redfield Jamison. New York City: The Free Press, 1993.

p. 15   *In a House of Dreams and Glass: Becoming a Psychiatrist.* Robert Klitzman. New York City: Simon & Schuster Trade, 1995.

p. 16   *Is There a Science of Behavior.* George Von Hilsheimer. Orange City, FL: Humanitas Curriculum, 1970.

p. 17   *The Psychoanalyst and the Artist.* Daniel Schneider. Ann Arbor, MI: Books on Demand, 1950.

Portraits of the Artist: Psychoanalysis of Creativity and Its Vicissitudes. John Gedo. Hillsdale, NJ: Analytic Press, 1989.

p. 18   *Stranger on the Earth: A Psychological Biography of Vincent van Gogh.* Albert Lubin. New York City: Henry Holt & Company, 1987.

p. 19   In *You Can Beat Depression: A Guide to Prevention and Recovery.* John Preston. Atascadero, CA: Impact Publishers, 2001.

p. 20   "The Neurobiology of Depression." Charles B. Nemeroff. *Scientific American* 278.6 (June 1998): 42–49.

CHAPTER 2

p. 40   *Dear Theo: The Autobiography of Vincent van Gogh.* Irving Stone. New York City: N A L, 1969. All van Gogh citations are from *Dear Theo.*

p. 41   *Fragments of a Journal.* Eugene Ionesco. New York City: Grove/Atlantic, 1968.

p. 43   *Man's Search for Himself.* Rollo May. New York City: Dell Publishing, 1973.

p. 44   *Reflections.* Hermann Hesse. New York City: Farrar, Straus & Giroux, 1974.

CHAPTER 3

p. 55   In *Muses from Chaos and Ash: AIDS, Artists, and Art.* Andrea Vaucher. New York City: Grove/Atlantic, 1993.

CHAPTER 4

p. 66   "Experimental and Clinical Treatments of Writing Blocks." Robert Boice. *Journal of Consulting and Clinical Psychology* 51.2 (April 1983): 183–91.

CHAPTER 5

p. 79   In *Personality, Spirit, and Ethics: The Ethics of Nicholas Berdyaev.* Howard Slaatte. New York City: Peter Lang Publishing, 1997.

p. 82   In *The Crisis in Modernism: Bergson and the Vitalist Controversy.* Frederick Burwick and Paul Douglass. New York City: Cambridge University Press, 1992.

p. 87   *The Pursuit of Meaning: Viktor Frankl, Logotherapy, and Life.* Joseph Fabry. Abilene, TX: Viktor Frankl Institute of Logotherapy, 1987.

CHAPTER 6

p. 91   In *Great Thinkers of the Eastern World.* Ian McGreal. New York City: HarperCollins Publishers, 1995.

        Resistance, Rebellion, and Death. Albert Camus. New York City: Random House, 1995.

p. 98   *The Myth of Sisyphus and Other Essays.* Albert Camus. New York City: Vintage Books, 1991.

CHAPTER 7

p. 105 In *Creativity in Human Development: An Interpretive and Annotated Bibliography.* A. Reza Arasteh and Josephine Arasteh. Rochester, VT: Schenkman Books, 1976.

p. 107 *Man's Search for Himself.* Rollo May. New York City: Dell Publishing, 1973.

p. 110 In *Anecdotes of Modern Art: From Rousseau to Warhol.* Donald Hall and Pat Corrington Wykes. New York City: Oxford University Press, 1990.

p. 111 In *Anecdotes of Modern Art: From Rousseau to Warhol.* Donald Hall and Pat Corrington Wykes. New York City: Oxford University Press, 1990.

p. 112 *Becoming: Basic Considerations for a Psychology of Personality.* Gordon Allport. New Haven, CT: Yale University Press, 1955.

CHAPTER 8

p. 125 In *Writer's Yearbook Extra, 2001.* Cincinnati: F & W Publications, 2001.

CHAPTER 9

p. 128 *The Thirsty Muse: Alcohol and the American Writer.* Tom Dardis. New York City: Houghton Mifflin Company, 1989.

p. 130 In *Heroes, Rogues, and Lovers: Testosterone and Behavior.* James McBride Dabbs. New York City: McGraw-Hill, 2001.

p. 132 *At Seventy: A Journal.* May Sarton. New York City: W. W. Norton & Company, 1984.

p. 133 *The Misfits: A Study of Sexual Outsiders.* Colin Wilson. New York City: Carroll & Graf Publishers, 1989.

p. 134 In *The Existential Imagination.* Frederick Karl and Leo Hamalian. New York City: Premier Books, 1976.

Witness to the Fire: Creativity and the Veil of Addiction. Linda Schierse Leonard. Boston: Shambhala Publications, 1989.

p. 135 In *Creativity and Madness: Psychological Studies of Art and Artists.* Barry Panter, et al. Sherman Oaks, CA: A I M E D, 1994.

CHAPTER 10

p. 139 *Narcissism and the Psychotherapist.* Sheila Welt and William Herron. New York City: Guilford Publications, 1990.

p. 142 *Psychopathology: A Case Book.* Robert Spitzer. Burr Ridge, IL: McGraw-Hill Higher Education, 1983.

p. 144 "Working with Partners of Performing Artists." Jennifer Sils. *Progress: Family Systems Research and Therapy* Summer 1992.

p. 145 "Further Contributions to the Understanding of Stage Fright: Narcissistic Issues." G. O. Gabbard. *Journal of the American Psychoanalytic Association* 31.2 (1983): 423–41.

"Stage Fright in Musicians: A Psychodynamic Perspective." Julie Nagel. *Bulletin of the Menninger Clinic* 57.4 (1993): 492–503.

p. 147 *Self and Others: Object Relations Theory in Practice.* N. Gregory Hamilton. Northvale, NJ: Jason Aronson Publishers, 1991.

CHAPTER 11

p. 155 *The Artist in Society.* Lawrence Hatterer. New York City: Grove/Atlantic, 1965.

p. 157 Original article, prepared for *Treating the Muse.* Eric Maisel. In manuscript.

CHAPTER 12

p. 166 *Significant Others: Creativity and Intimate Partnership.* Whitney Chadwick and Isabelle de Courtivron. New York City: Thames & Hudson, 1993.

In *Significant Others: Creativity and Intimate Partnership.* Whitney Chadwick and Isabelle de Courtivron. New York City: Thames & Hudson, 1993.

p. 167 In *Significant Others: Creativity and Intimate Partnership.* Whitney Chadwick and Isabelle de Courtivron. New York City: Thames & Hudson, 1993.

p. 167 In *Anecdotes of Modern Art: From Rousseau to Warhol*. Donald Hall and Pat Corrington Wykes. New York City: Oxford University Press, 1990.

p. 173 In *Significant Others: Creativity and Intimate Partnership*. Whitney Chadwick and Isabelle de Courtivron. New York City: Thames & Hudson, 1993.

CHAPTER 13

p. 192 In *Creativity*. Philip Vernon. New York City: Penguin Books, 1971.

p. 193 *The Meaning of It All: Thoughts of a Citizen Scientist*. Richard P. Feynman. New York City: Perseus Books Group, 1999.

CHAPTER 14

p. 198 *Women Music Makers: An Introduction to Women Composers*. Janet Nichols. New York City: Walker & Company, 1992.

CHAPTER 15

p. 211 *Art and Artist: Creative Urge and Personality Development*. Otto Rank. New York City: W. W. Norton & Company, 1989.

p. 214 In *Beethoven: Letters, Journals and Conversations*. Michael Hamburger. New York City: Thames & Hudson, 1992.

p. 216 In *Existentialism from Dostoevsky to Sartre*. Walter Kaufmann. Magnolia, MA: Peter Smith Publisher, 1984.

The Art of Living: The Classic Manual on Virtue, Happiness, and Effectiveness. Epictetus. Translated and adapted by Sharon Lebell. San Francisco: HarperSanFrancisco, 1995.

p. 217 *Mirrors of Man in Existentialism*. Nathan Scott. Nashville: Abingdon Press, 1980.

INDEX

ABOUT THE AUTHOR

I look forward to receiving your feedback on *The Van Gogh Blues*, and I'd love to hear from you about your experiences with creativity, depression, meaning-making, and the other issues presented in this book. The best way to reach me is to visit www.ericmaisel.com and send me an e-mail from my Web site. You may also be interested in obtaining my free monthly e-mail creativity newsletter, to which you can subscribe when you visit the site. Thank you!

Dr. Eric Maisel is a licensed family therapist, creativity coach, and creativity coach trainer with a doctorate in counseling psychology and master's degrees in creative writing and counseling. As a bestselling author, he's written more than 20 works of fiction and nonfiction, including *Artists Speak, Fearless Creating, A Life in the Arts,* and *Sleep Thinking*. He is a regular contributor to *Writer's Digest*, writes a monthly column for *Art Calendar* magazine, and maintains a private creativity coaching practice in San Franscisco.